VOCABBUSTERS
SAT Vol. 1
revised edition

VOCABBUSTERS
SAT Vol. 1
revised edition

Dusti D. Howell, Ph.D.
Deanne K. Howell, M.S.

ISBN 9780967732886

Printed in the United States of America

Authors:	Dusti D. Howell, Ph.D.
	Deanne K. Howell, M.S.
Illustrators:	James E. Rinehart II
	Brad Williams
Cover Design:	Another Design Guy, LLC
Book Layout:	Tracey Paramore

SolidA, Inc.

Address:	1717 Sherwood Way
	Emporia, KS 66801
email:	info@solida.net
Internet:	http://www.solida.net

About the Authors

Dusti D. Howell, president of SolidA, has a Ph.D. in Educational Communications and Technology and a Ph.D. minor in Educational Psychology from the University of Wisconsin-Madison. Much of his research was done at Emporia State University as an Associate Professor in the Instructional Design and Technology Department. His expertise also includes innovations and research in high-tech study skills and digital learning strategies. Dusti has taught every grade level from first grade to graduate school.

Deanne K. Howell has earned a Masters Degree in Curriculum and Instruction from the University of Wisconsin-Madison. She is also an educator with experience teaching elementary through graduate classes.

Dusti and Deanne have published numerous books and articles, and have developed a number of workshops and multimedia programs.

SolidA, Inc. is dedicated to improving student learning with technology and scientific research. Our passion is to help learners succeed. Our goal is to help students get Solid A's.

Special Acknowledgments

We would like to express our sincere gratitude to:

Jim Rinehart and Brad Williams who brought humor and life to our words through their cartoon illustrations.

John C. Lehman, Communications Professor at Emporia State University, for generously donating his time and talent to the audio recordings.

Brenda Gray, for her work with the voice narrations.

Merriam-Webster, Incorporated for permission to use their written pronunciations throughout this book.

Julie Rosenquist and Ginger Lewman for their input and advise on this project.

Tracey Paramore for her help with the design layout.

We also thank Rachel Haskins and Cecelia White for their assistance.

Table of Contents

Fun while learning vocabulary?

Vocabbusters introduces new words using a fun, multisensory approach.

* Each word is illustrated with a cartoon.
* Memory devices (mnemonics) are used to help you further remember and learn each word.
* Understand how each word is used in context with example sentences taken from major books and publications.
* Avoid mispronunciations by listening to the audio recordings.
* Enjoy watching select words come to life with clever animations that are sure to make you smile.
* Crossword puzzles, Matching Activies, and Multiple Choice Quizzes are included for review.
* Make up your own vocabulary cards by using the VOCABBUSTERS template at the back of this book.
* Learn how to search GoogleBooks to find your own words used in context.

For more free resources visit, http://www.solida.net

Introducing the VOCABBUSTERS Methodology

Learning vocabulary does not have to be difficult or dull. VOCABBUSTERS is based on over two decades of research on vocabulary acquisition, retention and usage. The strategies used in this book have been statistically proven to be superior learning devices for building vocabulary. VOCABBUSTERS combines two of the best methods to assist you in learning new words—the Keyword and Semantic-Context methods. The presentation of this information, centered on a cartoon, creates a memorable visual mnemonic. Audio recordings enable students to hear the words in order to pronounce the words correctly. Kinesthetic activities help to make learning easier and more fun.

Why is having a good vocabulary important?

Vocabulary acquisition is the single best indicator of intelligence and IQ according to Robert Sternberg, an Educational Psychologist at Yale University. Extensive portions of college entrance exams, including the S.A.T. and G.R.E., use vocabulary testing as a measure to predict academic performance. More importantly, simply reading does not guarantee a good vocabulary (Sternberg, 1986), which means that strategies for acquiring vocabulary need to be taught. Unfortunately, most schools do not devote any time for teaching effective techniques for learning vocabulary. When learning new vocabulary words, most students are left to rely on rote memorization, unaware that more efficient strategies are available. Therefore their vocabulary suffers, and in the end, many students remain ill prepared for college, and subsequently become more limited with their career choices.

VOCABBUSTERS is Simply the Best!

There are two simple reasons why VOCABBUSTERS is the best method for learning new vocabulary words. First, VOCABBUSTERS is two scientific methodologies built into one. By combining two of the most empirically validated methods for learning vocabulary into one simple interface, we have significantly increased the learner's chances for success. Second, we have added visual, auditory and kinesthetic supports to allow learners multiple "brain based" pathways for learning new words. That means you can study with just your strongest sensory style, or you can utilize all three sensory modalities. It all depends on what works best for you. For example, an auditory learner can just listen to the online audio files, or s/he can study the visual cartoons and easily utilize the kinesthetic techniques to quickly find dozens of example sentences online and then write a favorite one down at the bottom of each page. Again, our purpose is to easily provide the tools to allow you to study in the way that best suits your style of learning, thereby increasing your chances for success. Let's take a look at the two reasons why VOCABBUSTERS is the best in greater detail.

1) Combing the Best Methods

Numerous research articles have been written to prove the veracity of one method over another. It is interesting to note that in these "Battles of the Methods" two methods have been studied in great detail—the Keyword and Semantic-Context methods. In much of the research, the keyword method was shown to be very strong and empirically the best method for learning new vocabulary. However, over time, studies have shown semantic-context to be an excellent method, and in some cases as good as the keyword approach. A more detailed analysis of the strengths and weaknesses of each method led to an interesting discovery. The major strengths of each method complemented and added value to the other method. By juxtapositioning (combining) these two methods, the user will be able to easily remember definitions (keyword strength) and apply them in daily communications (semantic-context strength). For years these methods have been battling it out to see which one is the best. It is almost like comparing peanut butter and jelly. However, by combining the two methods into one new method, VOCABBUSTERS gives students a stronger base of research on which to rely.

The Keyword Method

The first step in using this method is to find a keyword for the word you are trying to learn. For example, let's say you're trying to learn the word *olfactory*. A good keyword for the word *olfactory* is *oil factory* because it follows three rules.

1. The word sounds acoustically similar to the target word.
2. The word is a concrete noun, which makes it easier to draw or visualize.
3. The word is common or familiar to the learner.

The second step is to link the keyword to the target definition. More simply, we need to link the word *oil factory* to "sense of smell." Visualize watching smoke spewing from an oil factory and smelling really bad. Draw a simple picture that depicts this situation and add the caption "That *oil factory* is bothering my *olfactory* sense." This visual mnemonic will assist the learner in remembering the meaning of the new word.

The final step is to practice recalling the target word. When you think of *olfactory*, first think of the keyword (*oil factory*), then remember what was happening in the picture (smoke is spewing out and smells bad), and finally that *olfactory* means *sense of smell.*

When tested against other methods, the keyword strategy repeatedly proved to be a superior technique for acquiring vocabulary for subjects of nearly all ages, and with periodic review, one of the best methods for long-term retention. The strength of this mnemonic strategy is in aiding the learner in remembering the definition of vocabulary words. Mnemonic strategies work! In fact, Purdue University researchers' Mastropieri and Scruggs (1991), "never found a 'type of learner' who could not benefit from mnemonic instruction." Additionally, the subjects in these studies not only liked the use of the strategy but expressed greater enjoyment in learning.

Semantic-Context Method

To learn a word using this method, context clues are placed in the sentence to help the learner define the word. For example, try to figure out what olfactory means from the following sentence. "His *olfactory* sense told him that someone had been smoking in the room." Clues within the sentence help the user define the meaning as "the sense of smell."

The semantic-context method has been identified as one of the best learning devices and has tested as one of the best strategies for delayed recall. Strictly speaking, in this book, only the first example sentence uses the semantic-context method. We created these sentences so that the target words were used within a meaningful context. We added two additional sentences from print sources that demonstrated real life examples. Although some of these sentences could also be considered semantic-context, only the first example sentence was strictly created for that purpose. These sentences as a whole should aid learners in actively integrating these words into their working vocabulary, using them on a daily basis.

2) Study with Style

What's your cognitive style? Do you learn best when you see an illustration depicting the meaning of a new word (visual), when you hear the new word being used (auditory), or when you find an example of the word used in real life and write it down (kinesthetic)? By providing visual cartoons, audio narrations and kinesthetic activities, we allow users to study with their primary learning styles. Keyword mnemonics create excellent visual links connecting keywords to the definitions of the targeted vocabulary word. This visual approach is best for recalling word definitions. We created the audio from the caption sentences of the cartoons and from each semantic-context sentence (first example sentence for each word). Auditory learners should find these extremely helpful in learning these words. Finally, kinesthetic learners can follow the directions on page fourteen to quickly find dozens of example sentences online and then write a favorite one down at the bottom of each page.

Many will certainly find it useful to integrate all three of these approaches into the learning process for each word. By listening to the recordings while reading over the sentences and studying the cartoon, and then searching through lists of example sentences and selecting one to write down, users will be storing this information in multiple locations of their brain. Proponents of dual coding theory claim that multimedia enhanced lessons can help strengthen the learning process by processing the same information in multiple areas of the brain, including the visual and auditory cortexes. Even more than dual coding, perhaps those that use all three approaches are using triple coding. Either way, every one of these supports is given with the goal of giving learners multiple methods to succeed.

VOCABBUSTERS Caters to all Types of Learners.

Here's how VOCABBUSTERS engages the three primary senses in learning new words.

> ### What's Your Cognitive Style?
> Find out free at www.solida.net

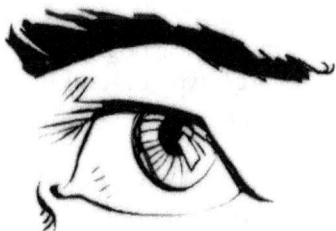

Visual Learners learn best when they see a visual image or picture. The cartoon illustrations for each word create a humorous and memorable way for learning new words. When trying to recall the meaning of a word, visual learners should try to remember the keyword and the related cartoon that illustrates the word. Recalling the activity in the cartoon helps visual learners remember the meaning of the target word. Additionally, visual learners might find it beneficial to color the pictures in the book.

Auditory Learners- Audio files increase learning and eliminate the guess work from determining pronunciations. Students no longer need to worry about whether they are mispronouncing words. According to middle school teacher Ginger Lewman, "I've had kids work on

words by themselves and come back to me mispronouncing them. For instance, the word facade (pronounced f&-'säd) becomes f&-'kAd. Now that could be VERY embarrassing on down the road and discourage them from trying to learn new words on their own." With the audio recordings, auditory learners can easily learn new words independently and pronounce them correctly. Students with auditory preferences can review words by listening to them at any time.

Watch and listen to select words come to life in funny animated cartoons at http://www.solida.net.

Kinesthetic Learners- Interact with the words by creating additional example sentences for each word. A great way to do this is to use *Google Books*. Google Books is a completely free online search engine that enables users to search inside books for pages that include a particular word. Here's how to use this valuable tool:

1. Go to Google's Books website at http://books.google.com.
2. If you are searching for the word **baleful**, type **baleful** in the Google Search Books window and press "Search Books."
3. Pick your favorite sentence from this list and write it in the "write your own" section provided at the bottom of the page.

Use the VOCABBUSTERS template at the back of this book to make your own "VOCABBUSTERS" or visit http://www.solida.net to print it from a PDF file.

For additional kinesthetic activities solve the crossword puzzles and take the matching and multiple choice quizzes at the end of the chapters. Also try to Listen to the recordings while moving about.

Pronunciation Guide

Many words have more than one correct pronunciation. In this book we have included one or two of the most common pronunciations for each word.

(http://www.m-w.com/cgi-bin/dictionary#)

\&\ as **a** and **u** in **a**b**u**t	\ᵊ\ as **e** in kit**te**n	\&r\ as **ur/er** in furth**er**
\a\ as **a** in **a**sh	\A\ as **a** in **a**ce	\ä\ as **o** in m**o**p
\au\ as **ou** in **ou**t	\ch\ as **ch** in **ch**in	\e\ as **e** in b**e**t
\E\ as **ea** in **ea**sy	\g\ as **g** in **g**o	\i\ as **i** in h**i**t
\I\ as **i** in **i**ce	\j\ as **j** in **j**ob	\[ng]\ as **ng** in si**ng**
\O\ as **o** in g**o**	\o\ as **aw** in l**aw**	\oi\ as **oy** in b**oy**
\th\ as **th** in **th**in	\[th]\ as **th** in **th**e	\ü\ as **oo** in l**oo**t
\u\ as **oo** in f**oo**t	\y\ as **y** in **y**et	\zh\ as **si** in vi**si**on

By permission of the publisher. From Merriam-Webster's Online Dictionary at http://www.merriam-webster.com by Merriam-Webster, Incorporated.

How to Review

Try to recall as much information about each word before looking at the page. You may wish to cover up the page, with only the target vocabulary word visible. Try to recall each part before uncovering it. To review the word *olfactory*:

1. Recall the keyword [oil factory]
2. Visualize the cartoon picture of the sun inhaling the fumes from the smelly oil factory.
3. Connect the picture to the meaning of the target word [referring to the sense of smell]
4. Think about how the word was used in a sentence or try to make up a sentence of your own.

VOCABBUSTERS Sample Overview

❶ Olfactory

❷ äl-'fak-t&-rE, Ol-'fak-trE⁺

❸ (Adjective) referring to the sense of smell

❹ Keyword: oil factory

❺

HOWELL OIL

❻ The smelly fumes from the **oil factory** bothered my **olfactory** sense.

❼ His **olfactory** sense told him that someone had been smoking in the bathroom.

❽ Little boys have been giggling about outhouses and their accompanying **olfactory** assaults since, well, caveman days.[A]

Finally, it was my nose that was the judge of land. It came to my **olfactory** sense, full and fresh, overwhelming: the smell of vegetation. I gasped. After months of nothing but salt-water-bleached smells, this reek of vegetable organic matter was intoxicating.[B]

❾ write your own: |

© Solida, Inc.   http://www.solida.net

1. Target word
2. Pronunciations are from the experts at Merriam-Webster. Many words have more than one pronunciation.
3. Part of speech and definition.
4. The keyword consists of a word or short phrase that sounds similar to the target word.
5. Cartoon illustration links the target word to the keyword and definition.
6. The cartoon caption ties the target word to the keyword and definition.
7. The target word used within a meaningful sentence (Semantic Context).
8. Two example sentences taken from leading books or publications.
9. Create your own sentence using the target word. Use the directions on page xii to find great example sentences.

Section One

a-b&-'rA-sh&n

(Noun) something unusual; different from the typical
Keyword: a bear nation

The approval of **a bear nation** by the United Nation Council (which previously consisted only of humans) was an **aberration**.

After receiving straight A's for two years, his parents hoped that his poor report card was just a temporary **aberration**.

For those under 30, space travel is now something taken completely for granted, the Challenger shuttle disaster of 1986 a dim **aberration** of long ago....[1]

It's easy to write this off as an **aberration**. The Timberwolves won't shoot 63% through three quarters on too many nights....[2]

write your own:

Abet

'&-'bet

(Verb) to actively aid or help (usually
in some wrongdoing)
Keyword: a bet

By distracting the dealer, the cheater **abetted** his buddy in
stealing a few coins during **a bet**.

Camille wisely refused to **abet** her friends in shoplifting.

In the story ... a wacky cast of estate workers and locals ...
aid and **abet** the conspiracies, disasters and love affairs of
the family.[3]

[In the human body] redundant mechanisms have evolved to
ensure that fuel is conserved as fat to **abet** survival in lean
times....[4]

write your own:

Abstinence

'ab-st&-n&nts or ab-st&-n&ns

(Noun) self-denial, especially resistance to tempting foods or alcoholic beverages

Keyword: absent

Jim's **abstinence** from fatty food was maintained by being routinely **absent** from the dinner table.

The doctor ordered total **abstinence** from alcohol as it could interfere with the prescribed medicine.

Total **abstinence** during the holidays is not recommended, even by weight loss specialists.[5]

Convinced that **abstinence** is the only solution to alcohol abuse, they maintain their mandate for unhealthy drinking habits....[6]

write your own:

Abstruse

&b-'strüs or ab-'strüs

(Adjective) difficult to comprehend; obscure
Keyword: abscessed tooth

With an **abscessed tooth**, the professor's **abstruse** lecture became even more difficult to understand.

The physics professor had a way of making **abstruse** concepts simple and easy to understand.

Breaking news from the world of particle physics tends to be greeted with a great big "Huh?" ... Theories of how the tiniest bits of matter and energy interact left the realm of common sense decades ago and are now wrapped up in **abstruse** mathematics and mind-bending terminology.[7]

Understanding the concept is not all that difficult. It's the math part ... that makes it all seem so **abstruse**.[8]

write your own: |

Acquiesce

"a-kwE-'es

(Verb) to comply unwillingly
Keyword: yak for less

He finally **acquiesced** and sold his **yak for less** than he originally wanted.

After hours of begging to go to the party, her parents finally **acquiesced** and told her she could.

No one, of course, thought the Milwaukee Bucks would go 82-0. Then again, no one should have expected them ... to **acquiesce** so meekly to the rampaging Minnesota Timberwolves.[9]

Powell wrote in his memoirs of Vietnam, "I vowed that when our turn came to call the shots, we would not quietly **acquiesce** in half-hearted warfare for half-baked reasons that the American people could not understand or support."[10]

write own:

Aesthetic

es-'the-tik or is-'the-tik

(Adjective) relating to what is beautiful or attractive
Keyword: athletic

With rippling muscles and a lean physique, the **athletic** javelin thrower has an **aesthetic** appearance.

The townspeople petitioned to have the building demolished, claiming it had little **aesthetic** value.

They leave unsightly junk cars to accumulate around the property. RVs, boats, and trailers also can create **aesthetic** problems.[11]

My friend took it in stride, providing generous amounts of fabric and making **aesthetic** improvements—more sparkles, a bigger star on the wand, etc—to her son's great and often delirious satisfaction.[12]

write your own:

&-'fi-n&-tE

(Noun) a likeness or fondness for
someone or something
Keyword: a fin

George has such an **affinity** for sharks that he is attracted
to **a fin** every time he sees one.

Most people naturally have a strong **affinity** for whales and
will travel thousands of miles to see them.

Unable to figure out a way to break into the entertainment
business, he opened an auto repair shop in Forestville. But
he kept looking for ways to tap into his **affinity** for music.[13]

He felt a natural **affinity** with ... the art of others through
history that have used their creative powers to express and
support their ideals.[14]

write your own: |

Aloof

&-'lüf

(Adverb) uninvolved
(Adjective) unfriendly or distant
Keyword: a roof

Not wanting to get involved in the family quarrel, he sat **aloof** on **a roof**.

Because he showed little interest in what anyone was doing, his peers could not determine if the **aloof** student was shy or arrogant.

He can come across as distant and somewhat **aloof**, yet there's nothing dispassionate about the way [he] guides his ... team.[15]

She cites the common view that this "island nation" has always held **aloof** from the continent. Nonsense, she says, reminding us that, while Britain has often fought against continental powers, it has usually done so in alliance with other continental powers.[16]

write your own:

Amalgamate

&-'mal-g&-"mAt

(Verb) to unite or join into one
(especially groups or organizations)
Keyword: animal gate

The zoo animals had to **amalgamate** into one group at feeding time to go through the **animal gate**.

The school dropped its band program and **amalgamated** its members into the orchestra when they lost their band leader.

He declined to approve the charter granted by Dongan, and at once sought to **amalgamate** all of the colonies north and east of the Delaware River into a dominion of New England.[17]

The tomb's peculiar form may have resulted from an attempt to **amalgamate** the architectural features of three different civilizations....[18]

write your own:

Ameliorate

&-'mEl-y&-"rAt or &-'mE-lE-&-"rAt

(Verb) to improve a situation or condition
Keyword: meal rate

The **meal rate** was lowered to $1.00 to **ameliorate** the hunger of the poor.

The library's severe financial crisis was **ameliorated** when a local donor stepped forward and contributed a significant amount of money.

Every governmental attempt to **ameliorate** poverty seems to attract its own breed of parasite and leech.[19]

A report published by cancer research UK marks growing excitement among scientists over the potential of medicinal mushrooms to boost the immune system of cancer patients, to combat tumors, and to **ameliorate** the harsh side effects of radiotherapy and chemotherapy.[20]

write your own: |

'A-mE-&-b&l

(Adjective) friendly or agreeable
Keyword: Amy's stable

At **Amy's stable**, all of the horses are **amiable** and friendly.

Although Kristin is generally **amiable**, she can be unpleasant when she has not had enough sleep.

Doss is an **amiable**, soft-spoken, extremely thoughtful man....[21]

Parrots can be unpredictable. One generally **amiable** sulphur-crested Cockatoo named Tommy ... took umbrage when a friend of his owner began to wear glasses. After due reflection, he reached up and bit the man on the lip.[22]

write your own: |

Animosity

"a-n&-'mä-s&-tE

(Noun) strong, often active hostility or resentment
Keyword: Animal City

There is a lot of **animosity** in **Animal City**. The animals would rather kill each other than live together.

Despite the rigorous competition between the teams, there is no **animosity** among the players.

Wittily written, this follows a predictable path as Annabel's **animosity** turns to tolerance, then acceptance.[23]

The Devils will next play the Lightning, a team with whom they have no postseason history but perhaps some **animosity**, based on how penalty-filled their last two games were.[24]

write your own: |

Antagonist

an-'ta-g&-nist

(Noun) foe, opponent, or adversary

Keyword: ant tag

The **antagonistic** ant was far too aggressive in the game of **ant tag**.

The **antagonist** in a novel is often the most interesting character, creating problems and obstacles for others in the story.

It's rare in Tallahassee when environmentalists and developers agree, but Monday these historical **antagonists** joined to support a bill that could protect manatees and speed up permits for new boat docks.[25]

When Evans returned to New York City for a talk show appearance in 1992, her **antagonist** again confronted her at the studio. Guards hustled him off, and soon after, the terrified Evans fled back to Los Angeles.[26]

write **own:**

©Solid A, Inc.   http://SolidA.net

Arbiter

'är-b&-t&r

(Noun) a person who mediates or judges

Note: same as arbitrator

Keyword: orbiter

An **arbiter** was hired to mediate all of the disputes between the astronauts on the **orbiter**.

Because the two students could not talk to each other without getting into a fight, the teacher served as an **arbiter** while they discussed their problems.

A new exhibition of the royal wardrobe, to which the queen has given her blessing, pays homage to the accessories that have won her acclaim from many **arbiters** of style....[27]

He dominated all aspects of [the city's] public life, and he was the final **arbiter** of virtually every piece of government policy.[28]

write **own**:

&-'sA&l or &-'sAl

(Verb) to assault violently
Keyword: a sail

Pirates can easily **assail a sail** by ripping it to shreds.

Although John was cleared of all wrongdoing, he was still **assailed** by insults and abuse from his neighbors.

Rarely did Lincoln **assail** his subordinates for a loss in battle. Rather, he tended to stand by his commanders, offering them support and giving them encouragement.[29]

Will he march upstairs to Bob or Martin and tell them something erroneous about you or, worse, something true? These will be the questions that **assail** you in the cold, dark night....[30]

write your own: |

Atrophy

'a-tr&-fE

(Noun) wasting away; a progressive decline
(Verb) to be reduced in size and power
Keyword: a trophy

His body clearly **atrophied** 50 years after posing for **a trophy**.

The power of the government was in a serious state of **atrophy** when it could no longer stop the internal fighting within the country.

The study found that moderate drinking not only did not protect against stroke, but it also was associated with brain **atrophy**, presumably the result of brain cell death.[31]

Managers of agencies whose missions might be vital but unrelated to homeland security worry.... Their budgets might **atrophy**, and their work-force shrivels.[32]

write your own:

o-'ster or o-'stir

(Adjective) unadorned; simple; sparse/ harsh or severe
Keyword: a steer

The plain **steer** was **austere** with few markings on its hide.

The jail cell was an **austere** place with barren walls and no windows.

Theater tickets were cheap, even for those on an **austere** budget like hers.[33]

The woven profusion of curves and garlands and the color scheme, which ranges from gold to dusty rose, contrasts with the startlingly **austere** white of the ceiling....[34]

write your own: |

Baleful

'bAl-f&l or bA&l-f&l

(Adjective) harmful, with evil intention
Keyword: bale full

With **baleful** intent, Roger placed sneezing powder in the **bale full** of hay to make the cows miserable.

Her **baleful** stares sent shivers throughout my body. I could detect the evil intentions and the hatred in her eyes.

Martin Gilbert, the assiduous historian of Nazi crimes, turns in "The Righteous" toward the better side of the story, the record of those virtuous men and women who came to the rescue of Jews in the **baleful** years of 1940-45.[35]

The big lynx was not cooperating. Tipped gently from his metal crate onto a meadow near the Rio Grande Reservoir, he cast a **baleful** look at the people chattering in front of him—and growled.[36]

write own:

bi-'ll

(Verb) to misrepresent or expose something as false

Keyword: bee lied

The **bee lied** to the bear, in order to **belie** the vast amount of honey to be found in the hive.

All the beauty pageant contestants had calm and collected looks on their faces that **belied** the nervousness and excitement they were feeling before the winner was announced.

Greenville's small size and low-key attitude **belie** a thriving business center with a flourishing downtown....[37]

Tampa Bay Buccaneers coach Jon Gruden knows one effect of his addiction to coaching: those bags under his eyes that **belie** the fact he won't turn 40 until this summer.[38]

write your own: |

Belittle

bi-'li-t&l

(Verb) to regard as unimportant
Keyword: bee little

Bees in the hive **belittled** the **little bee** by making him feel small and unimportant.

Although she worked hard on her science project, the students **belittled** Jane for her messy presentation.

While it's important to reassure your child when she's frightened or upset by an imaginary incident, be careful not to **belittle** or make fun of her.[39]

The governor routinely **belittles** the Republicans' work, and they in turn openly ridicule his grasp of the legislative process.[40]

write your own:

Section 1 Crossword Puzzle

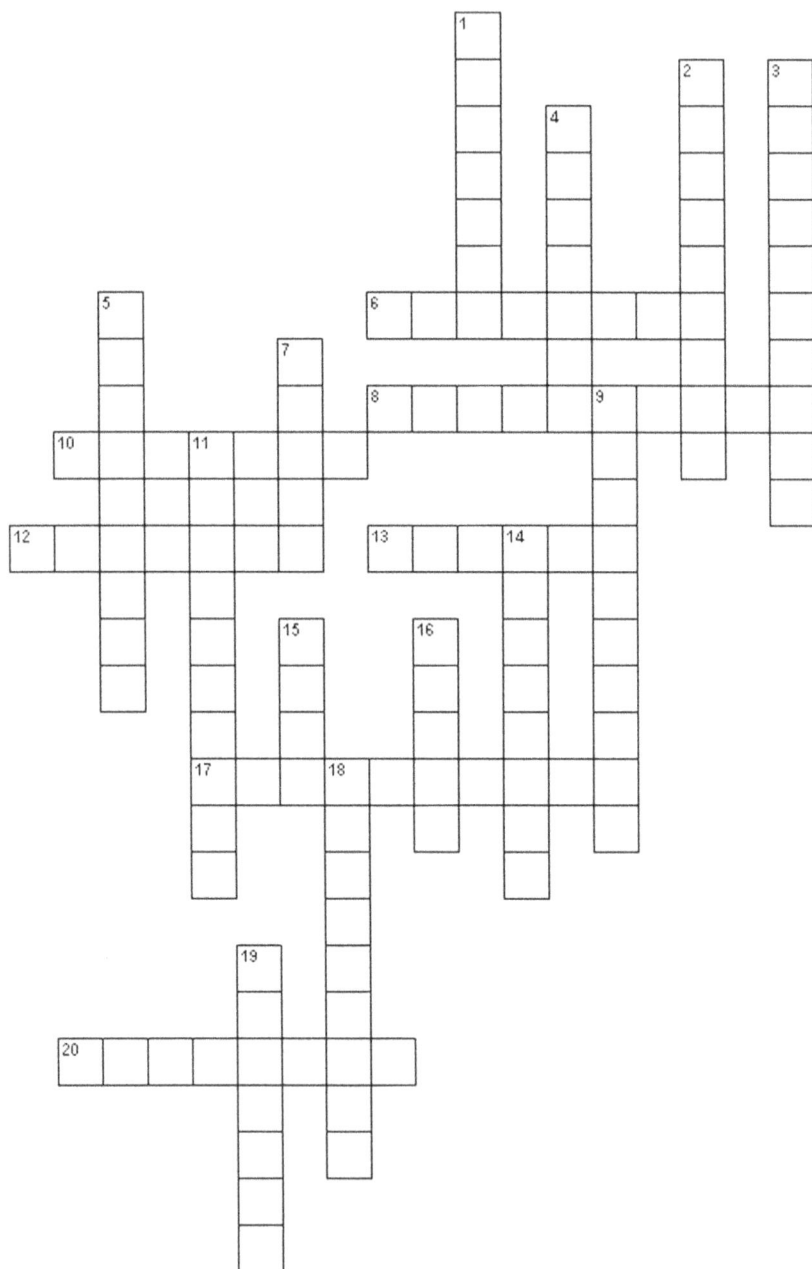

©Solid A, Inc.   http://SolidA.net

Across

6. to regard as unimportant

8. something unusual; different from the typical

10. friendly or agreeable

12. unadorned; simple; sparse/ harsh or severe

13. to assault violently

17. foe, opponent, or adversary

20. difficult to comprehend; obscure

Down

1. harmful, with evil intention

2. relating to what is beautiful or attractive

3. self-denial, especially resistance to tempting foods or alcoholic beverages

4. a person who mediates or judges

5. strong, often active hostility or resentment

7. to misrepresent or expose something as false

9. to unite or join into one (especially groups or organizations)

11. to improve a situation or condition

14. a likeness or fondness for someone or something

15. to actively aid or help (usually in some wrongdoing)

16. uninvolved/ unfriendly or distant

18. to comply unwillingly

19. wasting away: a progressive decline/to be reduced in size and power

Section 1 Multiple Choice Review

Fill in the blank with the best answer.

1. It is no wonder Samuel is spending the rest of his life in jail, with the _____ influence of his friends, he didn't have much of a chance.
    a. abstruse   b. amalgamated   c. baleful   d. belittled

2. The mere title of the book Michelle found at the library was so _____ that she had no clue what it was about.
    a. austere   b. aloof   c. amiable   d. abstruse

3. Bill harbored a feeling of bitter _____ toward Janet ever since she lied and got Bill in trouble.
    a. animosity   b. belittlement   c. affinity   d. abstinence

4. No longer able to maintain his _____ from fatty foods, Joe ate an entire bag of potato chips and half a gallon of ice cream.
    a. animosity   b. abstinence   c. affinity   d. aberration

5. After years of poverty and malnutrition, his body was in a condition of irreversible _____.
    a. affinity   b. aberration   c. belittlement   d. atrophy

6. Interior decorators gifted with a(n) _____ touch are able to choose colors and furniture styles that transform ordinary rooms into elegant works of art.
    a. aesthetic   b. antagonistic   c. austere   d. arbiter

7. The football team's crushing victory over last year's state champion team was a(n) _____ from the team's long string of losses.
    a. atrophy   b. aberration   c. antagonist   d. aesthetic

8. When he realized that the entire situation was a misunderstanding, the _____ in the dispute promptly apologized.
    a. arbiter   b. abstinence   c. antagonist   d. aberration

9. Many news reports _____ what is really going on in some foreign countries.
    a. belie   b. abet   c. assail   d. acquiesce

10. Because of severe rations, many people lived a(n) _____ existence during the Great Depression.
a. aesthetic   b. aloof   c. abstruse   d. austere

11. Sandy _____ her friends in the bank robbery by driving them to the bank.
a. ameliorated b. acquiesced c. amalgamated d. abetted

12. Charlie strongly disliked Pedro, but both boys were surprisingly _____ during the picnic.
a. aloof   b. amiable   c. abstruse   d. acquiesced

13. Although many of his friends were in the debate club, he kept _____ from any debates.
a. belied   b. amalgamated   c. ameliorated   d. aloof

14. The preschoolers had a strong _____ for the baby animals at the petting zoo and wanted to hold them.
a. abstinence   b. animosity   c. affinity   d. atrophy

15. When it started to rain during the garden party, the hostess _____ the situation by opening her home to the guests where it was warm and dry.
a. acquiesced   b. ameliorated   c. abetted   d. assailed

16. The performance was so bad that the actor was _____ with boos and criticism.
a. abetted   b. ameliorated   c. acquiesced   d. assailed

17. Columbus _____ to the demands of his crew and agreed to return to Spain if they did not find land within three days.
a. acquiesced   b. amalgamated   c. belied   d. assailed

18. People often _____ themselves for making simple mistakes.
a. amalgamate   b. belie   c. ameliorate   d. belittle

19. Jane was the _____ for her siblings and tried to help them resolve their arguments before her mother got involved.
a. aesthetic   b. animosity   c. arbiter   d. aloof

20. As part of a large renovation process taking place at the university, four different offices will be _____ into one main office that will serve the students' needs more efficiently.
a. abetted   b. amalgamated   c. atrophied   d. acquiesced

Section 1 Matching Review

Match the word on the left to the correct meaning on the right.

1. _____ Aberration
2. _____ Abet
3. _____ Abstinence
4. _____ Abstruse
5. _____ Acquiesce
6. _____ Aesthetic
7. _____ Affinity
8. _____ Aloof
9. _____ Amalgamate
10. _____ Ameliorate
11. _____ Amiable
12. _____ Animosity
13. _____ Antagonist
14. _____ Arbiter
15. _____ Assail
16. _____ Atrophy
17. _____ Austere
18. _____ Baleful
19. _____ Belie
20. _____ Belittle

A. something unusual; different from the typical
B. wasting away; a progressive decline/ to be reduced in size and power
C. foe, opponent, or adversary
D. harmful, with evil intention
E. self-denial, especially resistance to tempting foods or alcoholic beverages
F. to unite or join into one (especially groups or organizations)
G. relating to what is beautiful or attractive
H. to improve a situation or condition
I. a person who mediates or judges
J. unadorned; simple; sparse/ harsh or severe
K. difficult to comprehend; obscure
L. a likeness or fondness for someone or something
M. to actively aid or help (usually in wrongdoing)
N. uninvolved/ unfriendly or distant
O. to misrepresent or expose something as false
P. strong, often active hostility or resentment
Q. to assault violently
R. friendly or agreeable
S. to regard as unimportant
T. to comply unwillingly

Section Two

bi-'reft

(Adjective) being without something
that is needed or wanted
Keyword: theft

The museum was **bereft** of many artifacts and looked strangely empty after the **theft**.

Phillip stood frozen in front of his class, **bereft** of words, after he was asked to give an impromptu speech.

Without assistance, African governments cannot afford spraying programs [to kill mosquitoes], leaving them **bereft** of a safe, effective, and cheap defense [from malaria].[41]

Bereft of good leadership, they are trapped in needless bickering....[42]

write your own:

Blithe

'blIth

(Adjective) happy; lighthearted
Keyword: blind

The Three **Blind** Mice were so happy and cheerful that they changed their name to Three **Blithe** Mice.

Had Jim understood the dangers of the mountain, his **blithe** attitude about climbing may have been more serious.

[Princess Diana] could be unnervingly **blithe** even when talking about the most intimate and difficult periods of her life.[43]

Marketing is getting savvy, too, with one ad showing a man and woman sitting in airline seats, he loaded down with several volumes of print books, she sitting **blithely** holding a paperback-book sized reader. The point being that all the books the guy is holding can be loaded onto the itty-bitty reader. [44]

write your own: |

Bombastic

(Adjective) using words that sound important
in order to appear smarter
Keyword: bomb blast

The **bomb blast** expert's news conference sounded impressive, although no one understood his **bombastic** speech.

The **bombastic** preacher used Greek and Hebrew words throughout his sermon to try to increase his credibility.

I could have said that he was **bombastic** and loved the sound of his own voice, but that was not true.[45]

The second source of fury is the authors' **bombastic** style in describing power lawyers. A few examples will suffice: "twin towers of ambition and acquisitiveness," "supportive of the employer's macho-militant posture," "well-paid peddlers of influence."[46]

write own:

Boor

'bur

(Noun) a person lacking manners or taste;
a rude person
Keyword: burr

After stepping on the pokey **burrs** with her barefoot, Sally became such a **boor** that no one wanted to help her remove them.

David was considered a **boor** because of his tactless habit of speaking his mind and offending others.

The guy comes off as one insufferable, egotistical **boor**.[47]

George II is generally seen as a headstrong, blinkered [narrow-minded] **boor**, manipulated in his early years as king by his wife, Queen Caroline and by his chief minister....[48]

write your own: |

'brOch

(Verb) to open up; to mention a subject
Keyword: roach

WE NEED TO TALK ABOUT SANITATION!

After a **roach** was discovered in the restaurant kitchen, it was necessary to **broach** the topic of sanitation with the manager.

The room immediately fell silent when the sensitive subject that no one had yet dared to **broach** was finally brought up.

Yvonne has decided to **broach** the subject with Jotham. Rather than waiting until they're both upset, she's picked a time when they're relaxing on the couch.[49]

Some social democrats are also beginning to **broach** what has long been considered a taboo subject among their faithful.[50]

write your own:

Buffoon

"b&-'fün or b&-'fün

(Noun) a clown; an uneducated person
Keyword: balloon

That clown is such a **buffoon**. He's flying in the air popping all his helium **balloons**.

As a standup comic, my motto is not to be a **buffoon** unless I get paid for it.

He was a hero to many in his economically struggling district and a **buffoon** to those who watched his bizarre antics on the House floor and in Ohio courtrooms.[51]

John Lennon, unfaithful to Yoko and binging wildly on drink and drugs in the early 1970s, gets pegged as an infantile, self-involved **buffoon**.[52]

write own:

Cache

'kash

(Noun) secret stash; hiding place
Keyword: cash

The robber stashed the **cash** in his cactus **cache**—a secret hiding place resembling a cactus.

A **cache** of explosives remained hidden from the invading army.

Police found another pipe bomb yesterday in the same area where a **cache** of 14 were discovered in May.[53]

To her ... that means a Xerox that looks more like IBM, offering services to help businesses manage their vast **cache** of documents.[54]

write your own:

Cajole

k&-'jOl

(Verb) to persuade with gentle words/
to coax with false promises
Keyword: troll

The children tried to **cajole** the **troll** to let them cross the bridge.

Jessica discovered that if she **cajoled** her employees into completing tasks instead of threatening them, the job got done more quickly and with fewer mistakes.

"Go on, go on, go on...." Colman Conneely chanted a familiar refrain to **cajole** his brown mare into a faster trot.[55]

It is about a governor trying to woo, **cajole**, then threaten a legislative body for which he has long shown disdain, even when he served in its two houses.[56]

write your own: |

Capitulate

k&-'pi-ch&-"lAt

(Verb) to accept defeat unwillingly
Keyword: capture bait

The **captured bait capitulated** after the fisherman dug them up and ordered them to go to the bait stand.

Stephanie finally **capitulated** to the constant pleading of her friends and left her studies for a trip to the lake.

Motivated by love of his daughter and her future he **capitulates**, surrendering his own beliefs for her hopes.[57]

The fight for Baghdad could be more like a siege than a battle unless the Iraqis **capitulate** or President Bush changes his stated goals....[58]

write your own:

©Solid A, Inc.   http://SolidA.net

Catalyst

'ka-t&l-&st

(Noun) an agent that causes great change
Keyword: cattle

Farmer John's new jumbo milker was a **catalyst** for doubling the amount of milk produced by the **cattle**.

His poor report card was the **catalyst** for change. Now John is a straight A student.

The fire's **catalysts** were common pyrotechnic devices ... which are supposed to emit a shower of harmless sparks but instead ignited acoustic material on the club's walls and ceiling.[59]

In this sense, the manager role is the "**catalyst**" role. As with all **catalysts**, the manager's function is to speed up the reaction between two substances....[60]

write your own:

sh&-'grin

(Noun) distress or embarrassment caused by failure
Keyword: share a grin

Much to the actor's **chagrin**, the audience **shared a grin** when she accidentally tripped and fell on stage.

Imagine my **chagrin** when I realized that I had driven 200 miles in the wrong direction.

Years later, when Franklin was a world-famous figure, and Ambassador to France, he still remembered that the fact that he had paid too much for his whistle had caused him "more **chagrin** than the whistle gave him pleasure."[61]

[He] managed to pull in a 6-pound northern pike just 45 minutes after leaving the docks at 5 a.m., much to the **chagrin** of his wife [who perhaps had to cook it].[62]

write own:

Composure

k&m-'pO-zh&r

(Noun) calmness of mind or manner
Keyword: composer

While conducting his symphony, the **composer** stayed calm and retained his **composure** despite the verbal and physical assaults thrown at him.

John lost his **composure** and nearly started crying when he tripped on the stairs and dropped all of his books.

Anacondas do not resist being handled. But grab its neck and the snake's **composure** snaps.[63]

They regained their **composure**, possession game, and winning touch yesterday, just in time to launch them into early-season contention in the MLS Eastern Conference.[64]

write your own: |

Contrite

'kän-"trIt or k&n-"trIt

(Adjective) regretful of past behavior
Keyword: con fight

After the **con fight**, the prisoner felt **contrite** and apologized.

After realizing how hurtful she had been to her brother, Renee felt **contrite**.

We suspended him from school for a day. I've talked to him any number of times, and he's always **contrite** and promises to do better, but within a week, he's back at it again.[65]

When the year 2000 came and went without the arrival of Armageddon, or anyone being lifted up, Uncle Rulon explained to his followers that they were to blame, because they hadn't been sufficiently obedient. **Contrite**, the residents of Colorado City promised to live more righteously.[66]

write your own:

©Solid A, Inc.   http://SolidA.net

k&-'n&n-dr&m

(Noun) a question or riddle that is difficult to solve
Keyword: con and drum

Sherlock Holmes was brought in to solve the **conundrum** of the escaped **con and drum**.

Newlyweds are often faced with the **conundrum** of whose parents to visit during the holidays.

Countless scientific, technological and economic issues affect our understanding of the climate **conundrum** and our response to it.[67]

Since the book's launch in 2000, RS's fashion pages have been a **conundrum** for its two previous editors. Finding the right balance between sensible and stylish clothes has not been easy.[68]

write your own: |

Copious

'kO-pE-&s

(Adjective) large or excess amount
Keyword: soapiest

With his **copious** supply of soap, Jim enjoyed the **soapiest** bath in town.

The town had **copious** rain throughout the week, with flooding reported in many areas.

As I looked over all this stuff in my mind's eye my stomach began to cry out with hunger.... I salivated **copiously** and swallowed my saliva and began to belch deep, sour belches.[69]

Although the audit ... found **copious** flaws in the shelter's accounting system, the auditors did not point to any embezzlement, fraud, or other malfeasance [wrongdoing].[70]

write own:

Countermand

'kaun-t&r-"mand

(Verb) to annul; cancel/ make a contrary order
Keyword: counter man

Although the king's **counter man** was accurate, the king **countermanded** his total because he wanted to appear richer.

The substitute teacher **countermanded** all of our teacher's previous rules and allowed us total freedom in the classroom.

I've made up my mind, and none of you have the rank to **countermand** my order.[71]

Other Bush advisers say he might use a nonconfrontational approach to reach his goal—delay implementation of some of Clinton's recent initiatives ... until he believes the moment is right to **countermand** them permanently.[72]

write own:

Covert

'kO-"v&rt or 'k&-v&rt

(Adjective) hidden or secret
Keyword: covered

Stewart **covered** up the car when his friends came over to keep the restoration process a **covert** activity.

The U.S. government engages in many **covert** operations in which the general public is unaware.

In 1972, the Washington Post's revelation of the Watergate scandal led to public outcry about **covert** surveillance.[73]

[The cunning programming inserted into the algorithm] had been added in so shrewd a way that nobody, except Greg Hale, had seen it. Strathmore's **covert** addition, in effect, meant that any code written by Skipjack could be decrypted via a secret password known only to the NSA.[74]

write your own: |

Crass

'kras

(Adjective) insensitive or inconsiderate; stupid
Keyword: grass

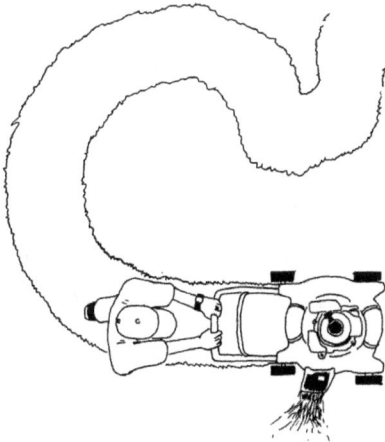

In spite of Mrs. Johnson's request for nice straight rows, Dan's **crass** attitude towards mowing the **grass** revealed that he did not care.

Putting your feet up so that the soles of one's feet or shoes are facing another person is considered highly offensive and **crass** in the Middle East.

They want to do something patriotic, but they don't want to do something that comes across as **crass**.[75]

This is too smart a market, say entrepreneurs, to be swayed by **crass** commercialism or false prophets.[76]

write your own:

Criterion

krI-'tir-E-&n or kr&-'tir-E-&n

(Noun) a standard to be judged by

Note: Criterion is singular, criteria is plural

Keyword: cry tears

She **cried tears** when she just missed the **criterion** for an A.

One **criterion** for getting into a top university is high academic achievement.

A few weeks ago, Mayor Tom Menino asked Boston to judge him by a single, severe **criterion**: the performance of our public schools.[77]

The winner's edge is not in a gifted birth, a high IQ, or in talent. The winner's edge is all in the attitude, not aptitude. Attitude is the **criterion** for success. –Denis Waitley.[78]

write your own: |

Daunt

'don't or 'dänt

(Verb) to discourage (someone);
to threaten or intimidate
Keyword: haunt

Although people tried to discourage Timothy from entering the **haunted** house, he was brave and did not feel **daunted**.

After a near accident during her first drive, Annie realized what a **daunting** experience driving could be.

Metastatic breast cancer, severe emphysema, three operations, and several weeks in the hospital did not **daunt** her spirit.[79]

The threats are myriad. The challenges facing our country **daunting**.[80]

write own:

Section 2 Crossword Puzzle

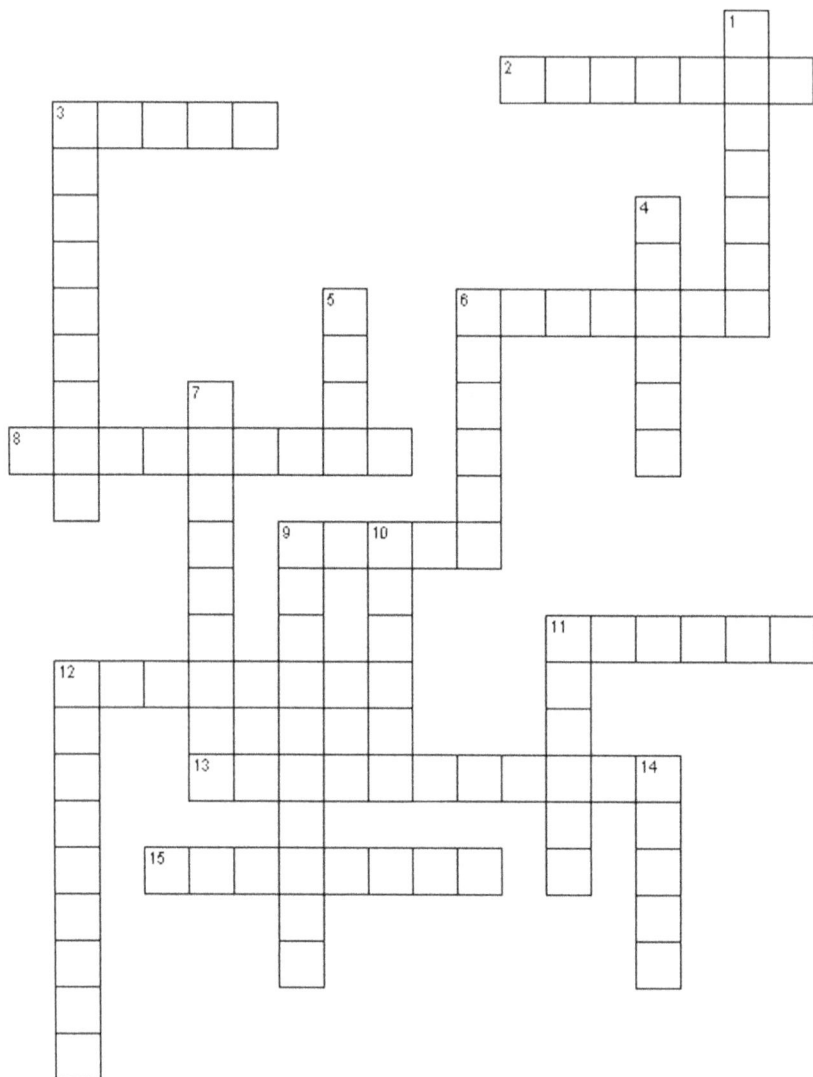

©Solid A, Inc.   http://SolidA.net

Across

2. large or excess amount

3. insensitive or inconsiderate; stupid

6. distress or embarrassment caused by failure

8. calmness of mind or manner

9. secret stash; hiding place

11. happy; lighthearted

12. regretful of past behavior

13. to annul; cancel/ make a contrary order

15. an agent that causes great change

Down

1. a clown; an uneducated person

3. a standard to be judged by

4. being without something that is needed or wanted

5. a person lacking manners or taste; a rude person

6. to persuade with gentle words/ to coax with false promises

7. using words that sound important in order to appear smarter

9. to accept defeat unwillingly

10. hidden or secret

11. to open up; to mention a subject

12. a question or riddle that is difficult to solve

14. to discourage (someone); to threaten or intimidate

Section 2 Multiple Choice Review

Fill in the blank with the best answer.

1. Cindy was not sure how to _____ the subject of her bad grades
   with her parents.
   a. countermand   b. cajole   c. broach   d. capitulate

2. Ryan was able to _____ his friends into helping him by making
   the offer seem too good to pass up.
   a. capitulate   b. cajole   c. buffoon   d. broach

3. Enzymes used in the experiment acted as a _____. They caused
   the reaction to happen more quickly without being changed themselves.
   a. catalyst   b. broach   c. buffoon   d. conundrum

4. Much to my _____, the mall was not open when I got there.
   a. bereft   b. chagrin   c. composure   d. conundrum

5. The _____pictures in the vacation brochure portrayed only the
   very best locations of the island.
   a. bombastic   b. chagrin   c. contrite   d. blithe

6. The Romanian judge's _____for a perfect 10 in gymnastics com-
   petitions at the Olympics are impossible to achieve.
   a. cache   b. catalyst   c. criteria   d. composure

7. Walking into a new classroom in a new school, Michelle was not at
   all _____.
   a. cajoled   b. daunted   c. bereft   d. capitulated

8. Jane regained her _____after hitting the wrong note while sing-
   ing.
   a. composure   b. criterion   c. chagrin   d. cache

9. Most of the employees considered the inconsiderate co-worker a
   _____and tried to steer clear of him at all costs.
   a. buffoon   b. conundrum   c. blithe   d. boor

10. Joe is such a _____ in class. He likes to gain attention by telling jokes.
   a. boor   b. broach   c. cache   d. buffoon

11. The children were _____ after lying to their parents, and wished they had told the truth.
   a. crass   b. contrite   c. covert   d. copious

12. The students felt Susan sounded _____, as she enjoyed bragging about her job using the technical jargon she used at work.
   a. bombastic   b. contrite   c. crass   d. composed

13. He kept all of his gold and diamonds in a _____ that no one could find.
   a. cache   b. conundrum   c. boor   d. broach

14. Middle East peace is a _____ that has been debated for decades.
   a. boor   b. catalyst   c. conundrum   d. countermand

15. My father got upset with my mother when she _____ his discipline by allowing us to go to the party even when we were grounded.
   a. capitulated   b. broached   c. countermanded   d. cajoled

16. After her dog passed away, Pam felt utterly _____ and lonely.
   a. contrite   b. bereft   c. copious   d. daunted

17. Preparation for Alice's surprise birthday party had to be kept as _____ as possible.
   a. crass   b. bereft   c. bombastic   d. covert

18. During the lectures, the teacher presented _____ illustrations and graphs on dozens of handouts.
   a. crass   b. blithe   c. copious   d. covert

19. His _____ remarks to the girls made them cry.
   a. crass   b. composed   c. bereft   d. chagrin

20. The president's advisor _____ after being harassed by the general public to resign from his position.
   a. countermanded   b. capitulated   c. cajoled   d. daunted

Section 2 Matching Review

Match the word on the left to the correct meaning on the right.

1. _____ Bereft
2. _____ Blithe
3. _____ Bombastic
4. _____ Boor
5. _____ Broach
6. _____ Buffoon
7. _____ Cache
8. _____ Cajole
9. _____ Capitulate
10. _____ Catalyst
11. _____ Chagrin
12. _____ Composure
13. _____ Contrite
14. _____ Conundrum
15. _____ Copious
16. _____ Countermand
17. _____ Covert
18. _____ Crass
19. _____ Criterion
20. _____ Daunt

A. a standard to be judged by
B. to accept defeat unwillingly
C. an agent that causes great change
D. insensitive or inconsiderate; stupid
E. being without something that is needed or wanted
F. secret stash; hiding place
G. to persuade with gentle words/ to coax with false promises
H. calmness of mind or manner
I. using words that sound important in order to appear smarter
J. distress or embarrassment caused by failure
K. a person lacking manners or taste; a rude person
L. to open up; to mention a subject
M. regretful of past behavior
N. happy; lighthearted
O. to annul; cancel/ make a contrary order
P. a question or riddle that is difficult to solve
Q. a clown; an uneducated person
R. hidden or secret
S. to discourage (someone); to threaten or intimidate
T. large or excess amount

Section Three

'd&rth

(Noun) scarce or inadequate supply or amount
Keyword: dirt

> DON'T GO NEAR THE EDGE! THERE IS ALREADY A DEARTH OF EARTH HERE!

Because there was a **dearth** of **dirt** on the island, the castaways stayed away from the edge to avoid knocking more ground into the ocean.

A **dearth** of food left the small village near starvation.

For students, these requirements are considered "very few, almost nonexistent." As one sophomore describes it: "The **dearth** of requirements really allows the student to pursue any academic venture unimpeded...."[81]

[The director at] the Future of Music Coalition, which recently produced a devastating study of the **dearth** of diversity in the radio industry, says it is time to start thinking about the fight for media democracy ... as a winnable one.[82]

write your own: |

Debacle

dE-'bä-k&l or de-b&-k&l

(Noun) a breakup; an overthrow;
a sudden great disaster
Keyword: the buckle

Television stations were given hefty fines after televising the great Grammy **debacle** when a movie star showed up wearing only **the buckle**.

The fund raising car wash ended up being the biggest **debacle** in the school's history after two cars were stolen out of the parking lot.

Like a supercriminal, he can winch himself in and out of a filmic **debacle** before anyone knows....[83]

The service is slow, the drinks weak, and the food tastes like ripe garbage. You have two options during this painful experience. Option A: Critique the restaurant and smugly point out to your partner how wrong he or she was and how this **debacle** could have been avoided if only you had been listen to. Option B: Shut up and eat the food.[84]

write your own:

Decadence

'de-k&-d&nts or di-'kA-d&ns

(Noun) deterioration in social and moral behavior

Keyword: deck of dents

The **deck of dents** which was smashed with a sledge-hammer was proof of his **decadence**.

The dark ages were synonymous with the **decadence** of the arts and sciences—a period when people went to great lengths to destroy books or artifacts.

Crime and moral **decadence**, Americans tell themselves, are the worrisome signposts of social decline.[85]

From their experiences in Europe, the Founding Fathers knew that a lax approach to personal behavior leads to **decadence** and decay.[86]

write own:

Deference

'de-f&-r&nts or 'def-r&ns

(Noun) polite courtesy; respect
Keyword: deaf friends

Rob showed **deference** for his **deaf friends** by learning to speak to them in sign language.

John shows **deference** to his girl friend by opening her car door when they go out for a date.

He had the respect of everyone, and he was treated with **deference** in his evening practices.[87]

The species until very recently was known as the squawfish. ...The name was changed in **deference** to American Indian tribes, who find the word "squaw" offensive.[88]

write your own:

di-'li-nE-"At

(Verb) to indicate or describe/
to form the outer boundaries or outline of something
Keyword: deal on apes

The advertisement clearly **delineated** that the **deal on apes** would end at midnight.

The boundary of the basketball court is **delineated** by a thick black line.

This detailed artwork showcases the muscles used during each exercise and **delineates** how these muscles interact with surrounding joints and skeletal structures.[89]

What **delineates** the brilliant from the ordinary? Is it innovation or idiosyncrasy? Productivity or paradox?"[90]

write your own:

Demagogue

'de-m&-"gäg

(Noun) a leader who usually appeals to people's emotions and prejudices
Keyword: denim dog

As a fashion **demagogue**, the **denim dog** influenced his fellow dogs to wear denim.

The leader of the cult was a **demagogue** who preyed on the emotions and prejudices of his group.

[He had to] quell his own revulsion at some of the lines he had to speak in those scenes where the fledgling Nazi **demagogue** starts addressing political meetings and discovers his capacity for rousing the rabble with hatred and invective.[91]

And the world is full of **demagogues** who have gotten away with advancing stupid or dangerous ideas because they've wrapped themselves in the cloak of religion.[92]

write your own:

di-'m&r

(Verb) to express hesitation or objection
Keyword: lemur

Because he ate the same thing day after day, the **lemur demurred** when given bananas again.

Tom **demurred** and argued with his mother after she insisted that he clean his room.

The Dutch have a word for people who are particularly stubborn, who keep going against all the odds. They're called kaaskops—cheeseheads—and John Langen doesn't **demur** when the label is put on him.[93]

Most players **demur** when asked about winning postseason awards, reciting, as if on automatic pilot, "If the team does well, that will take care of itself.[94]

write your own:

Deprecate

'de-pri-"kAt

(Verb) to express disapproval about someone or something/ to speak of something as unimportant
Keyword: Debra's cake

Everyone **deprecated Debra's cake** at the wedding because it tasted as bad as it looked.

Feeling jealous of his sister's trophy collection, John **deprecated** her achievements.

In Washington, when an official wants to **deprecate** his knowledge of a given situation, he admits to being only "newspaper deep."[95]

While I stress the physical causes of PPD [Postpartum Depression], I don't mean to **deprecate** how stress, lack of sleep and fatigue can add to the illness.[96]

write own:

Derogatory

di-'rä-g&-"tOr-E

(Adjective) belittling; degrading
Keyword: your rug is sorry

Teasing the bald man with the toupee, she made the **derogatory** remark, "**Your rug is sorry**."

The students made very **derogatory** comments about the terrible taste of the cafeteria food.

I have never heard any **derogatory** comments about him. As a hockey player and gentleman, Jean Beliveau has no equal. –Coach Toe Blake[97]

Ed Burns is a jock. Not in any **derogatory** sense—it's just that the strapping 6-footer was a basketball player at Hunter College before he was an actor, writer and director, and he still carries himself with a muscular ease.[98]

write your own:

Despot

'des-p&t or 'des-pät

(Noun) dictator; ruler with unlimited power
Keyword: spit

The cruel and vicious **despot** didn't like his lunch so he **spit** on the cook before sending him to prison.

His step-father ruled the family like a **despot** with very strict punishments issued for even the smallest infractions.

Still hiding in the jungle nearly 20 years after being forced from power, it wasn't likely the deposed **despot** would ever give up his dream of ruling again.[99]

Judge John Henry McBryde ruled his court like a minor **despot**, angering lawyers and fellow judges. Now they're lined up to depose him....[100]

write your own: |

Diatribe

'dI-&-"trIb

(Noun) speech or writing
characterized by abusive criticism
Keyword: Diet Tribe

Before   Several Moons After

To avoid hearing another hour long **diatribe** about the tribe's excessive weight gain from the chief, the **Diet Tribe** began eating only vegetables.

The mother launched into a **diatribe** after her son failed to clean up his room. She angrily criticized him for his sloppy approach to life.

He pronounced that last word with infinite disgust. I stood dumbstruck as the **diatribe** continued, and Wendy came out, drawn by the commotion.[101]

She patiently listened to my **diatribe**, instinctively letting me vent.[102]

write your own: |

©Solid A, Inc.   http://SolidA.net

Diffidence

'di-f&-d&nts or 'di-f&-"dens

(Noun) unwillingness to speak or act because
of low self confidence
Keyword: different dance

Because of her **diffidence** towards the tango, Holly waited
for a **different dance** that she knew better.

After working out at the gym for several months, Jake became a more confident person, and his **diffidence** began to
disappear.

His voice was icy now, full of command. All the trembling
and **diffidence** gone.[103]

In fact, it was Howell's **diffidence**—an almost painful shy-
ness in public and in private—that made him such a powerful
antidote to Wilkins….[104]

write your own:

Diffuse

di-'fyüs

(Adjective) scattered/ (Verb) to pour out and disperse
Keyword: the fuse

Caution: Commonly mistaken for *defuse* meaning
"to make less dangerous or hostile"

After he lit **the fuse**, the firecracker exploded and **diffused** its parts across the open lot.

We could not detect where the voices were coming from. The **diffused** echoes sounded as if they were coming from five different directions in the cave.

The hope is that positive change in the workforce will **diffuse** into the wider community.[105]

I've personally discovered that lavender oil massaged on my temples will rid me of a headache, and that, instead of brewing another cup of caffeine when I need an energy boost, I can **diffuse** into the air an inhalation of essential oils to pick me up....[106]

write your own:

                      http://SolidA.net

Dilatory

'di-l&-"tOr-E or 'di-l&-"tor-E

(Adjective) causing delay or tending to procrastinate
Keyword: fill a story

Because she waited until the last minute to do her home-work, the **dilatory** student decided to **fill a story** with many adjectives in order to meet the page requirement for the assignment.

His **dilatory** approach to his morning routine made him con-stantly late for work.

To quash a filibuster [a tactic to delay legislation] ... Byrd arranged for then-Vice President Walter Mondale, the pre-siding officer of the Senate under the Constitution, to rule all **dilatory** amendments out of order.[107]

Sometimes the subject responds correctly but after a delay or in a **dilatory** manner. Often a sluggish response to com-mands is due to the fact that the subject has not been taught to respond quickly.[108]

write your own:

Discordant

'dis-"kor-d[&]nt

(Adjective) disagreeing; harsh sounding
Keyword: this cord

Pulling on the left cord chimes a pleasant sound. However, pulling on **this cord** will result in a loud **discordant** sound.

Though most reviews of the new restaurant were positive, there was one **discordant** review from a reporter who was displeased with the service.

Believe it or not, even very young babies notice whether music is harmonious or **discordant** and prefer harmonies.[109]

Better to go by the trees that sheltered the large colonies of fruit bats; the only assault there at that early hour was the bats' **discordant** concerts of squeaking and chattering.[110]

write your own: |

Disparity

di-'spar-&-tE

(Noun) dissimilarity; having different parts or elements
Keyword: this pair

There is a **disparity** with **this pair** of boots. The two boots are different sizes.

City officials are gravely concerned about the **disparity** in living conditions between the poor and rich citizens of their community.

The statistical **disparity** between the trio's regular-season and postseason efforts is striking.[111]

This difference between boys and girls at play epitomizes what Harvard's Carol Gilligan points to as a key **disparity** between the sexes: boys take pride in a lone, tough-minded independence and autonomy, while girls see themselves as part of a web of connectedness.[112]

write your own: |

Disposition

"dis-p&-'zi-sh&n

(Noun) a person's character or temperament
Keyword: in this position

George has a very happy and relaxed **disposition** when he is in this **position**—reclining in his favorite chair.

Sammy was born with a sunny **disposition**—always smiling and giggling.

Other benefits [of eating zucchini] include muscle strengthening, enhanced energy, clearer thinking, and a happier **disposition**.[113]

The fountain of content must spring up in the mind, and he who hath so little knowledge of human nature as to seek happiness by changing anything but his own **disposition**, will waste his life in fruitless efforts.... --Samuel Johnson[114]

write your own:

Distraught

dis-'trot

(Adjective) extremely troubled, concerned, or worried
Keyword: dish trot

When he saw his **dish trot** away with his spoon, he felt **distraught** and concerned about how he was going to eat.

The parents were **distraught** and worriedly paced the floor when their daughter did not come home by 11 p.m.

Last year, more than 10,000 teens came from all over China to audition to become the next veejay on MTV Mandarin. One finalist, who had traveled 18 hours to Beijing, was so **distraught** at losing that MTV offered to let her veejay for a day.[115]

The empress, **distraught** over her husband's death, died a few days later.[116]

write **own:**
your

'dä-s&l or 'dä-sIl

(Adjective) tame; willing to be taught
Keyword: fossil

The archeologists found **fossils** of **docile** pets of the ancient cave men.

Though the raccoon appeared **docile**, it immediately bared its teeth and growled when anyone approached its cage.

Three days later, **docile** and calm, Corbett presented himself to the relatives of the man he had attacked.[117]

During the day the meerkats were **docile** and harmless, but at night, under their collective weight, they crushed their enemies ruthlessly.[118]

write your own:

Dormant

'dor-m&nt

(Adjective) temporarily not active
Keyword: door mat

Sally removed the welcome **door mat**, and waited until her parent's anger was **dormant** before putting it out again for her friends.

Bobby's talent for art remained **dormant** for years until his grandmother bought him an easel and paints.

The great curving ramparts of the Bala Hisar Fort loomed over the receding town, glowing in the fiery light like a long-**dormant** volcano on the verge of awakening.[119]

The Ku Klux Klan lay largely **dormant** until 1915, when D.W. Griffith's film *The Birth of a Nation* (originally titled *The Clansman*) helped spart its rebirth.[120]

write your own:

Section 3 Crossword Puzzle

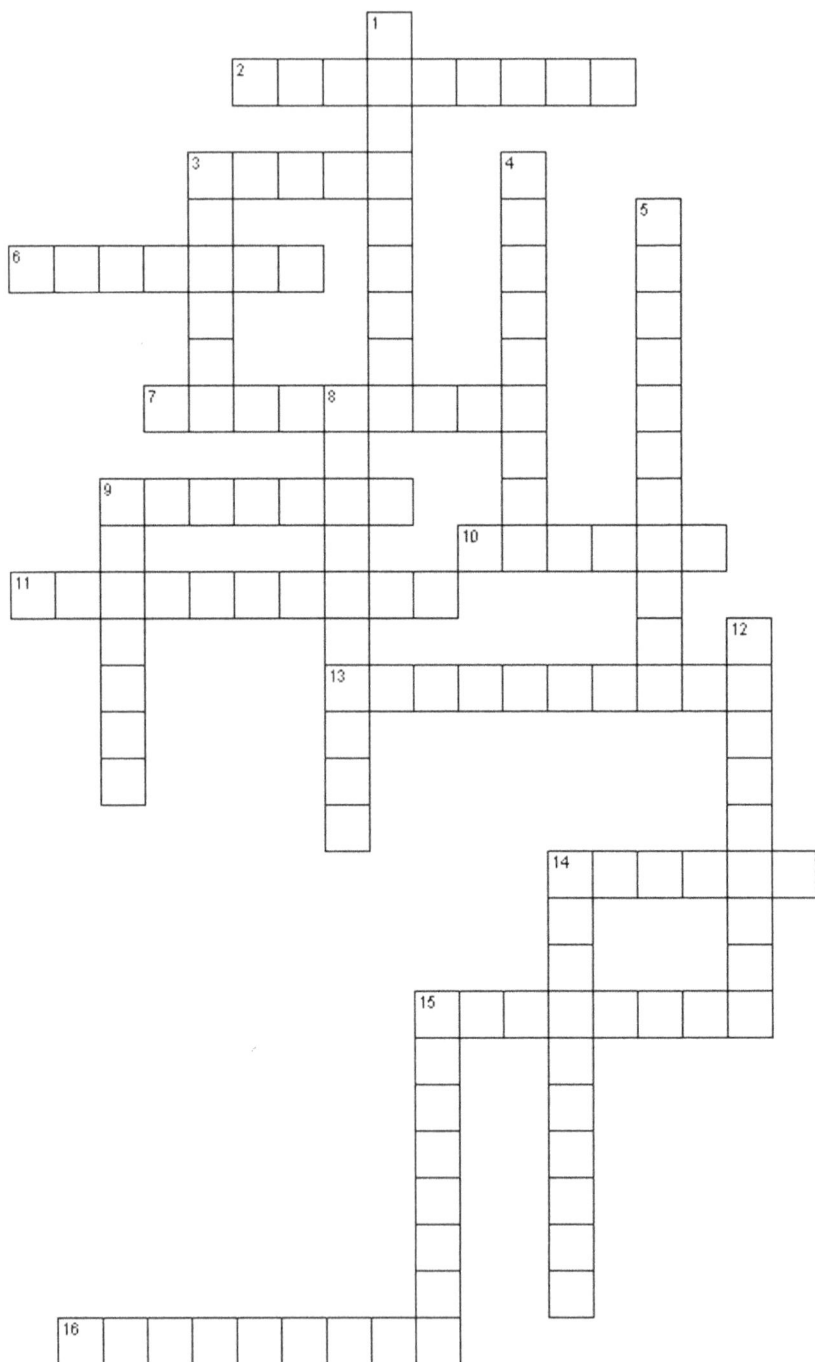

©Solid A, Inc.   http://SolidA.net

Across

2. polite courtesy; respect

3. to express hesitation or objection

6. a breakup; an overthrow; a sudden great disaster

7. deterioration in social and moral behavior

9. scattered/ to pour out and disperse

10. scarce or inadequate supply or amount

11. belittling; degrading

13. unwillingness to speak or act because of low self confidence

14. dictator; ruler with unlimited power

15. speech or writing characterized by abusive critic

16. dissimilarity; having different parts or elements

Down

1. to express disapproval about someone or something/ to speak of something as unimportant

3. tame; willing to be taught

4. to indicate or describe/ to form the outer boundaries or outline of something

5. a person's character or temperament

8. disagreeing; harsh sounding

9. temporarily not active

12. a leader who usually appeals to people's emotions and prejudices

14. extremely troubled, concerned, or worried

15. causing delay or tending to procrastinate

Section 3 Multiple Choice Review

Fill in the blank with the best answer.

1. Because there was such a great _____ of skill between the basketball teams, the Lions ran away with the game with a score of 120 to 39.
   a. disparity   b. dearth   c. delineation   d. debacle

2. Many old timers complain about the _____ of manners and good behavior in kids today.
   a. disparity   b. dearth   c. deference   d. debacle

3. The river clearly _____ the western boundary of the state.
   a. delinates   b. demurs   c. deprecates   d. diffuses

4. Historically, before their demise, many civilizations went through a period of moral _____.
   a. disposition   b. diffidence   c. decadence   d. demagogue

5. The brilliant _____ rocketed his way to political prominence by appealing to the emotions and prejudices of the people.
   a. despot   b. demagogue   c. debacle   d. diatribe

6. The new employee was _____ and absorbent, making him a great candidate for learning a lot about the company in a short amount of time.
   a. docile   b. dilatory   c. discordant   d. distraught

7. Even though she was required to take a foreign language at school, Lacey _____ because she had never been very good with learning new languages.
   a. delineated   b. deprecated   c. diffused   d. demurred

8. Germany's Hitler and Cambodia's Pol Pot are twentieth century _____, known for their brutality.
   a. debacles   b. diatribes   c. despots   d. demagogues

9. He complained that they were always making _____ remarks about how stupid he was.
   a. dormant   b. docile   c. distraught   d. derogatory

10. The pungent smell of the skunk _____ quickly throughout the air.
    a. diffused   b. deprecated   c. demurred   d. demurred

11. The girl wrote a lengthy _____ denouncing her boyfriend for his faults.
    a. despot   b. diatribe   c. demagogue   d. disposition

12. Maggie's _____ at the meeting led people to believe that she was stuck up, when in reality she was very timid.
    a. decadence   b. diffidence   c. deference   d. disparity

13. The overloaded truck had a _____ effect on the flow of traffic, causing the traffic to back up for miles.
    a. discordant   b. dilatory   c. distraught   d. deprecating

14. The basketball coach gave his player a _____ look after he scored a basket for the other team.
    a. dormant   b. docile   c. deprecating   d. demurred

15. The child was _____ when his dog ran away.
    a. dormant   b. dearth   c. discordant   d. distraught

16. When the opposing team shoed up in the stadium, _____ booing exploded from the crowd.
    a. diffident   b. decadent   c. dormant   d. discordant

17. The opening night of the restaurant might not have been such a complete _____ if the owner had taken just a couple of extra months to prepare for the big event.
    a. disposition   b. diatribe   c. dearth   d. debacle

18. In spite of her illness, Sally had a pleasant _____ during her stay in the hospital.
    a. disparity   b. dearth   c. disposition   d. debacle

19. The volcano was considered _____ until it erupted into a giant mushroom of smoke, fire, and ash.
    a. dormant   b. diffuse   c. discordant   d. docile

20. Out of _____ for their mother, the children prepared an elaborate meal for Mother's Day.
    a. decadence   b. diffidence   c. deference   d. disparity

Section 3 Matching Review

Match the word on the left to the correct meaning on the right.

1. _____ Dearth
2. _____ Debacle
3. _____ Decadence
4. _____ Deference
5. _____ Delineate
6. _____ Demagogue
7. _____ Demur
8. _____ Deprecate
9. _____ Derogatory
10. _____ Despot
11. _____ Diatribe
12. _____ Diffidence
13. _____ Diffuse
14. _____ Dilatory
15. _____ Discordant
16. _____ Disparity
17. _____ Disposition
18. _____ Distraught
19. _____ Docile
20. _____ Dormant

A. polite courtesy; respect
B. disagreeing; harsh sounding
C. a breakup; an overthrow; a sudden great disaster
D. tame; willing to be taught
E. scattered/ to pour out and disperse
F. to express hesitation or objection
G. dictator; ruler with unlimited power
H. deterioration in social and moral behavior
I. extremely troubled, concerned, or worried
J. dissimilarity; having different parts or elements
K. a leader who usually appeals to people's emotions and prejudices
L. temporarily not active
M. belittling; degrading
N. scarce or inadequate supply or amount
O. to indicate or describe/ to form the outer boundaries or outline of something
P. causing delay or tending to procrastinate
Q. speech or writing characterized by abusive criticism
R. to express disapproval about someone or something/ to speak of something as unimportant
S. a person's character or temperament
T. unwillingness to speak or act because of low self confidence

Section Four

e-'klek-tik or i-'klek-tik

(Adjective) selecting or choosing from various sources
Keyword: electric

Johnny powered his **electric** car using several **eclectic** energy sources including solar, nuclear, wind, and battery.

Raymond was baffled by her **eclectic** taste in music. She liked rock 'n roll, country, punk, reggae, and polka.

The four grand streets of Burns, Iroquois, Seminole, and Adams were lined with stately houses built in **eclectic** styles. Red-brick Georgian rose next to English Tudor, which gave onto French provincial.[121]

In fact, what the skyscrapers at the end of Manhattan represented is an immensely complex and **eclectic** civilization. New York City is the most cosmopolitan place in the history of the world....[122]

write your own:

Efficacious

"e-f&-'kA-sh&s

(Adjective) effective; capable of
producing the desired effect
Keyword: effective cages

His search for **effective cages** proved **efficacious** when
he discovered a model with a new lock that even Houdini
could not escape from.

The seat belt is an **efficacious** safety device that reduces the
number of personal injuries in accidents.

Both Beaton's Guide and my own dim memories of folk medicine held that [a] spider's web was **efficacious** in dressing
wounds.[123]

So the Prime Minister rose to his feet in the House of Com-
mons on March 18th and gave the least tender and most **efficacious** speech of his career.[124]

write your own:

Elucidate

i-'lü-s&-"dAt

(Verb) to clarify or make clear
Keyword: loser date

She quickly **elucidated** that her blind date was a **loser date** by screaming when she opened the door.

If you don't understand what is being taught, please ask your teacher to **elucidate** further.

He depicts the numbing helplessness and dissociation that people feel when inundated with news that informs but does not **elucidate**.[125]

[Benjamin Thompson known later as Count von Rumford] became the world's foremost authority on thermodynamics and the first to **elucidate** the principles of the convection of fluids and the circulation of ocean currents.[126]

write your own:

©Solid A, Inc.   http://SolidA.net

Embroil

im-'broi&l or im-'broil

(Verb) to involve in confusion or conflict
Keyword: boil

The chefs became **embroiled** in a dispute over whether to **boil** or broil the fish.

The reluctance of the factory to clean up the sewage could **embroil** them in a lawsuit with the local community.

Her father is determined not to **embroil** his family in a messy, high-profile murder case.[127]

Every true friend to this Country must see and feel that the policy of it is not to **embroil** ourselves with any nation whatsoever; but to avoid their disputes and politics; and if they will harass one another, to avail ourselves of the neutral conduct we have adopted. - President George Washington[128]

write your own: |

Encumber

in-'k&m-b&r

(Verb) to hinder; restrict motion/ burden
Keyword: cucumber

Carrying the **cucumber encumbered** the man so much, he was unable to walk with it very far.

Thanks to luggage wheels, fewer people are **encumbered** by the heavy baggage they take with them while traversing through airports.

By looking at boys in a narrow way and failing to recognize the gentle, creative, empathic sides of many boys, I believe that some teachers—though they may not consciously intend it—can seriously **encumber** the emotional and scholastic development of boys in their classes....[129]

She cuts through the clutter of details that **encumber** many conversations and focuses on the heart of the matter.[130]

write your own:

©Solid A, Inc.   http://SolidA.net

Enervate

'e-n&r-"vAt

(Verb) to weaken or unnerve;
to reduce the mental or moral vigor
Keyword: nerve

Caution: enervate is nearly the opposite of energize

After spending twenty-four continuous hours removing a tumor from the patient's entangled **nerves**, the surgeon felt **enervated** and wiped out.

The well conditioned basketball team's strategy was to continue to increase the tempo on both ends of the court in order to **enervate** the opposing team.

Huntington created a hierarchy of civilizations based upon climactic advantage or disadvantage: cool climates stimulate civilizational energies, while tropical climates **enervate**.[131]

[Barry Bonds yelled] "Man, I'm burned out!" And that was before the Giants played the kind of white-knuckle marathon against the Diamondbacks that **enervates** the winners as much as the losers.[132]

write your own:

in-'hants, in-'hans, or en-'hans

(Verb) to improve in any way

Keyword: hands

The sculptor's **hands enhanced** the beauty of the garden with a stunning sculpture of his hands.

In Julie's secret cookie recipe, extra vanilla is used to **enhance** the flavor.

Each year, over 20,000 Americans receive organ transplants that save or **enhance** their lives, but about 6,000 others die while waiting for a transplant.[133]

To the degree that our emotions get in the way of or **enhance** our ability to think and plan ... they define the limits of our capacity to use our innate mental abilities, and so determine how we do in life.[134]

write your own:

Enigma

i-'nig-m& or e-'nig-m&

(Noun) a puzzling riddle; something unexplainable
Keyword: In a wig ma?

"Is that you **in a wig, ma**?" It was a real **enigma** when ma
started wearing an oversized wig.

Even after hours of explanation, the math problem remained
an **enigma** to the class.

Domestic cats harbor their own mysteries, of course, but
sometimes the **enigma** lies more within owner than pet.[135]

Early in his rehabilitation, Lathrop couldn't keep from re-
flecting on the **enigma** that has plagued and inspired so many
artists and philosophers throughout the history of Western
art and thought—the question of human suffering under a
supposedly benevolent God.[136]

write your own: |

Epilogue

‘e-p&-”log or ‘e-p&-”läg

(Noun) a short section added to the end
of a speech or written work

Keyword: kept a log

Susan loved happy endings, and **kept a log** of the best **epilogues** from her favorite books.

At the very end of the book, the **epilogue** was the saddest part of the whole story.

The Alter High School football team's dream season had a heartbreaking final chapter, but the **epilogue** was a happy one for the Knights. Ed Domsitz was named Associated Press co-coach of the year in Division III, while [two] seniors ... also earned first-team All-Ohio honors.[137]

Spielberg's film footage of [Emilie's first visit to Oskar's grave in the movie *Schindler's List*] serves as the **epilogue** to his $23 million black-and-white epic.[138]

write your own:

                    http://SolidA.net

Erudite

'er-&-"dIt or 'er-y&-"dIt

(Adjective) learned; scholarly
Keyword: air tight

After years of research, the **erudite** scientists discovered a new **air tight** storage system that kept his hamburger fresh for months.

The **erudite** professional organization had strict criteria to ensure that all of its prospective members were well read, intelligent, and had earned recognition in their chosen field of study.

Some of us also have an inferiority complex about poetry, viewing it as an art that only the well-educated, literate, and **erudite** can appreciate.[139]

As the Astro's resident intellectual, Brad Ausmus isn't known for his tirades. He is, by nature, soft-spoken and thoughtful to the point of being **erudite**.[140]

write your own:

'yü-l&-jE

(Noun) a speech or writing that displays high praise
(usually for someone who died)
Keyword: you love me

During the **eulogy** at my funeral, you cried when you said **you love me**.

The nation wept during John F. Kennedy's **eulogy**.

Alan King remembers delivering the **eulogy** at a funeral where Milton Berle was among the mourners.[141]

"First in war, first in peace, and first in the hearts of his countrymen." -a **eulogy** at the funeral of George Washington[142]

write your own: |

Evanescent

"e-v&-'ne-s[&]nt

(Adjective) fade away; disappear; vanish
Keyword: heaven sent

Heaven sent an angel to tell me something, but the **evanescent** vision disappeared too quickly.

Great ideas are often **evanescent**. Before you have a chance to write them down, you have already forgotten them.

What is athletic greatness if it doesn't have contagious properties? Only as **evanescent** as the smoke of a fine cigar.[143]

And so film [is] by nature the most transparent and **evanescent** of art forms, the one best suited to revealing the motion of our lives....[144]

write your own: |

Exacerbate

ig-'za-s&r-"bAt

(Verb) to aggravate; to make worse

Keyword: exact bait

Caution: Not to be confused with exasperate or exaggerate

The storeowner **exacerbated** the already angry customers by providing them with **exact bait** by measuring each worm with a ruler.

The current agricultural problems were further **exacerbated** by the drought.

Pataki has vowed to veto the State Legislature's aid package, saying it would **exacerbate** the state's budget deficit.[145]

Anxiety is now believed to **exacerbate** diabetes by raising levels of the stress hormone cortisol, which regulates insulin and blood-sugar levels.[146]

write your own:

Exhortation

"ek-"sor-'tA-sh&n or eg-"z&r-'tA-sh&n

(Noun) encouragement; to move one to action by argument, advice, or request
Keyword: egg sort station

After dozens of bad eggs were returned to their store, the **exhortation** of the salesman to buy an **egg sort station** was quickly approved.

The magazine article included an **exhortation** encouraging consumers to recycle their newspapers.

His drawn brows and the deep furrow between them showed that he needed no **exhortation** to concentrate all his attention upon a problem....[147]

As she herself acknowledged, she found it impossible to write a short letter, and to John Quincy and Charles came pages dispensing vigorous, motherly **exhortations**. "Strive to excel," she urged Charles. "Anything worth doing was worth doing well, she reminded them."[148]

write your own: |

Exonerate

ig-'zä-n&-"rAt or eg-'zä-n&-"rAt

(Verb) to clear of guilt or blame
Keyword: eggs on her plate

After the food fight Jen was **exonerated** because she still had all of her **eggs on her plate**, proving she did not take part in the fight.

The owner's ex-wife was **exonerated** of all suspicion after it was revealed the house fire was caused by an electrical failure.

A disturbing number of the veterans of Watergate seemed only too willing to **exonerate** Clinton for conduct that eerily resembled Nixon's....[149]

He kept a private diary! Yes, a diary, in which he placed all the blame on his wife! He was determined to make sure that coming generations would **exonerate** him and put the blame on his wife.[150]

write your own:

©Solid A, Inc. http://SolidA.net

Expunge

ik-'sp&nj

(Verb) to erase or remove completely
Keyword: sponge

The cartoon character began to **expunge** his body with a **sponge** until he disappeared.

The janitor **expunged** the lecture notes from the chalkboard when she washed it clean.

If fish **expunged** (which means to destroy, obliterate or delete) their eggs, we wouldn't have a lot of fish around.[151]

To many, Rose essentially flushed away any chance of a Hall of Fame induction in 1989, when he agreed to a lifetime ban from baseball for betting on games when he was manager of the Cincinnati Reds. Baseball's all-time hit leader has since worked tirelessly to **expunge** his name from Major League Baseball's blacklist, to no avail.[152]

write your own:

Extricate

'ek-str&-"kAt

(Verb) to remove or free
(someone or something); to set free
Keyword: extra cage

Due to the large number of rabbits born in the spring, the zoo keeper **extricated** the rabbits from the **extra cages** by releasing them in the countryside.

It took the tow truck several hours to **extricate** the van from the snow bank.

He managed to **extricate** himself, and then fell into another, deeper, crevasse.[153]

How do we **extricate** our emotions, mind, body, and spirit from the agony of entanglement?[154]

write your own:

Fabricate

'fa-bri-"kAt

(Verb) to make up a story
Keyword: fabric

In order to increase the sales at the **fabric** store, Gail **fabricated** a story about how the fabric was woven by hand by women in a remote indigenous tribe.

Greg knew that he had to **fabricate** a good story to tell his parents about the tragic condition of the house, or else they would never leave him home alone for a weekend again.

When I had told everything I could safely **fabricate** [the interrogators] asked no more questions.[155]

When she proudly refused to let him **fabricate** a scandal about her, he had her blacklisted.[156]

write your own:

Fallacious

(Adjective) misleading; tending to deceive
Keyword: fillet of fish

The packaging on the **fillet of fish** was **fallacious** because it was actually thinly sliced chicken.

Though Kristin's speech was good, her research and reasoning were based on **fallacious** findings.

In the first few days of the war, both newspapers slanted their headlines in an attempt to bolster their **fallacious** predictions.... The situation was so egregious [conspicuously bad] that I actually got mad at the pulp fiction that was in my hands.[157]

To survive these ordeals the new idea must be correct, as the **fallacious** and unsound ones are destroyed by the attacks made upon them.[158]

write your own:

Fastidious

fa-'sti-dE-&s or f&-'sti-dE-&s

(Adjective) hard to please/ meticulous with details
Keyword: fast idiots

Not pleased with the selection of beverages offered at the drink station in the marathon, the **fast idiots** were extremely **fastidious** and refused to drink anything.

The **fastidious** guests did not like anything the hostess was serving.

In the past, the Times editorial page had been criticized for being ... too **fastidious**.[159]

Industry insiders say Williams, Aetna's chief of health operations, is **fastidious**, a nut for detail....[160]

write your own:

Section 4 Crossword Puzzle

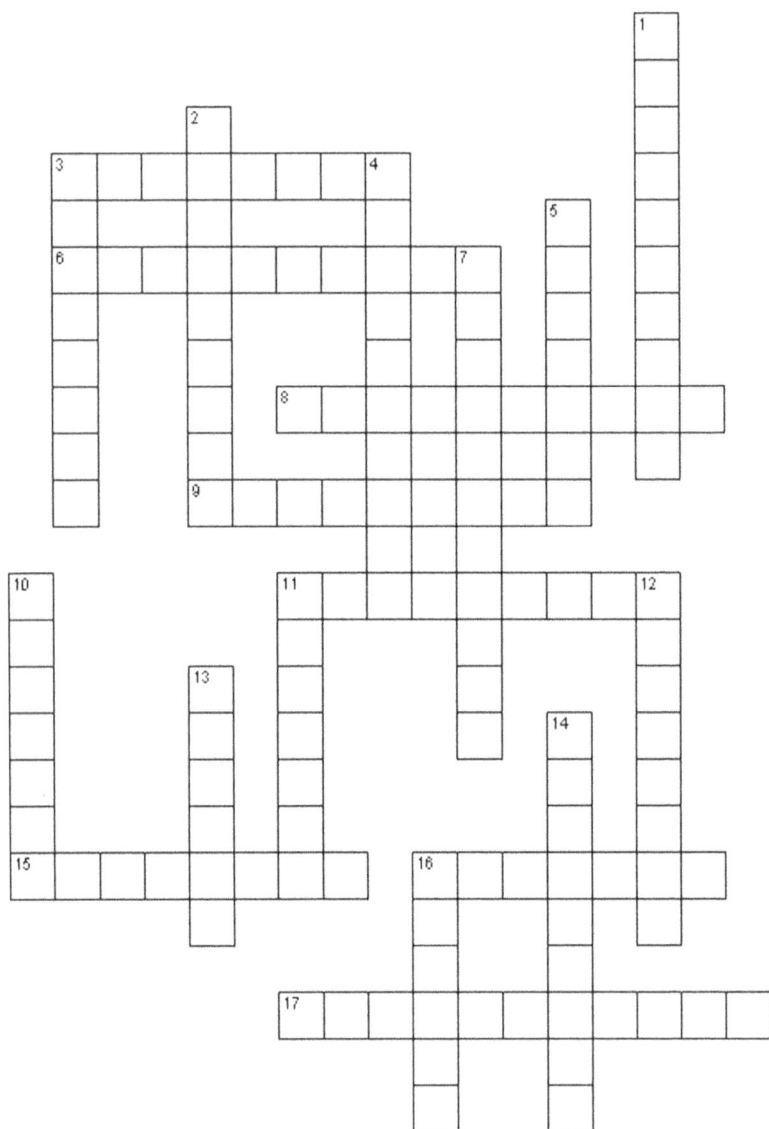

Across

3. a short section added to the end of a speech or written work

6. to aggravate; to make worse

8. hard to please/ meticulous with details

9. to clear of guilt or blame

11. to remove or free (someone or something)

15. to hinder; restrict motion/burden

16. to involve in confusion or conflict

17. encouragement; to move one to action by argument, advice, or request

Down

1. misleading; tending to deceive

2. to clarify or make clear

3. to weaken or unnerve; to reduce the mental or moral vigor

4. fade away; disappear; vanish

5. learned; scholarly

7. effective; capable of producing the desired effect

10. to improve in any way

11. to erase or remove completely

12. selecting or choosing from various sources

13. a puzzling riddle; something unexplainable

14. to make up a story

16. a speech or writing that displays high praise (usually for someone who died)

Section 4 Multiple Choice Review

Fill in the blank with the best answer.

1. By destroying his records, the criminal _____ the history of his crimes.
    a. elucidated   b. exonerated   c. extricated   d. expunged

2. The weight of the problems of the city _____ the mayor and visibly aged him while he held the office.
    a. encumbered   b. enhanced   c. elucidated   d. exhorted

3. The international students served an _____ cuisine from four continents at the banquet.
    a. embroiled   b. encumbered   c. eclectic   d. efficacious

4. The poor report card _____ the problems she was already having with her mother.
    a. enervated   b. fabricated   c. exacerbated   d. enhanced

5. After extensive testing, the drug proved to be _____ and was soon released into the drug market.
    a. efficacious   b. fallacious   c. evanescent   d. fabricated

6. The _____ director was picky in his attention to detail for the movie.
    a. fastidious   b. erudite   c. fallacious   d. eclectic

7. The student was _____ from cheating on the exam, after he proved he worked out the problems himself.
    a. encumbered   b. exonerated   c. enervated   d. expunged

8. Chris refused to get _____ with his best friend's fights.
    a. embroiled   b. fabricated   c. extricated   d. exonerated

9. After finding the perfect bicycle in a catalog, Wendy worked hard to _____ her allowance by doing additional chores.
    a. expunge   b. exacerbate   c. fabricate   d. enhance

10. It was rather an _____ why she broke up with him.
    a. epilogue   b. enigma   c. eulogy   d. erudite

11. The entire report regarding the condition of the store was
_____, including the names of the owners.
a. fallacious   b. fastidious   c. eclectic   d. efficacious

12. Kenny, the _____ professor, specialized in women's literature
and Shakespeare at the university.
a. fallacious   b. eclectic   c. fastidious   d. erudite

13. The oasis was a(n) _____ vision, disappearing as soon as the
wanderer reached the pool.
a. fallacious   b. evanescent   c. eclectic   d. fastidious

14. Despite the _____ of the owners to play somewhere else, the
neighborhood kids continued to loiter outside of the convenience
store.
a. exhortation   b. enigma   c. eulogy   d. epilogue

15. Scientists have _____ different hypotheses for the extinction of
the dinosaurs.
a. exacerbated   b. elucidated   c. fabricated   d. extricated

16. In an attempt to _____ the kite from the tree, Jeff ended up
tearing the kite.
a. enervate   b. embroil   c. extricate   d. encumber

17. Though everyone knew they were _____, we all enjoyed listening to Bill's stories about what he did over the weekend.
a. evanescent   b. erudite   c. efficacious   d. fabricated

18. During the reception, the author indicated to several people that
the _____ of her book was the most difficult part to write.
a. eulogy   b. epilogue   c. enigma   d. exhortation

19. The hot, humid air and the hard physical work _____ the teenagers so much they wanted to take a nap.
a. exacerbated   b. embroiled   c. enervated   d. elucidated

20. The newspaper editor had a tendency to _____ his stories about
famous people.
a. embroil   b. encumber   c. eulogize   d. enervate

Section 4 Matching Review

Match the word on the left to the correct meaning on the right.

1. _____ Eclectic
2. _____ Efficacious
3. _____ Elucidate
4. _____ Embroil
5. _____ Encumber
6. _____ Enervate
7. _____ Enhance
8. _____ Enigma
9. _____ Epilogue
10. _____ Erudite
11. _____ Eulogy
12. _____ Evanescent
13. _____ Exacerbate
14. _____ Exhortation
15. _____ Exonerate
16. _____ Expunge
17. _____ Extricate
18. _____ Fabricate
19. _____ Fallacious
20. _____ Fastidious

A. a puzzling riddle; something unexplainable
B. to erase or remove completely
C. a short section added to the end of a speech or written work
D. effective; capable of producing the desired effect
E. to clear of guilt or blame
F. a speech or writing that displays high praise (usually for someone who died)
G. hard to please/ meticulous with details
H. learned; scholarly
I. fade away; disappear; vanish
J. to hinder; restrict motion/burden
K. to improve in any way
L. to make up a story
M. to weaken or unnerve; to reduce the mental or moral vigor
N. encouragement; to move one to action by argument, advice, or request
O. to aggravate; to make worse
P. to remove or free (someone or something)
Q. selecting or choosing from various sources
R. misleading; tending to deceive
S. to involve in confusion or conflict
T. to clarify or make clear

Section Five

'fek-l&s

(Adjective) ineffective/ without care or responsibility

Keyword: freckles

John never bothered to use sunscreen. As a result of this **feckless** attitude, he ended up with lots of **freckles**.

Because Darlene was a **feckless** rider, she got bucked off of the horse.

Nelson personifies **feckless** slackerdom.[161]

Didn't dirty water come from the neglect of **feckless**, greedy governments?[162]

write own:

Fervor

'f&r-v&r

(Noun) intense and sincere emotion
Keyword: fever

Chris had such **fervor** for the team he even attended their games with a **fever**.

The coach's half time pep talk ignited **fervor** into the team.

Indeed, Nikonova got a lot of sound out of the instrument's [mandolin's] three strings, sometimes by rapidly strumming them but always by attacking them with **fervor** and precision.[163]

But he's no match for the villain of the piece … a cruel lazy parasite with a passion for women and gambling and the ability to charm unsuspecting parents with the **fervor** of his dedication.[164]

write your own: |

'flA-gr&nt or 'fla-gr&nt

(Adjective) scandalous; shocking; outrageous
Keyword: flag rent

The citizens were shocked and outraged by the city's new **flag rent** ordinance requiring all spectators to rent city flags for the parade at the **flagrant** price of $5 per hour.

The **flagrant** language of the politician offended many people and ended up costing him thousands of votes.

The evidence shows that the suggestion that she be removed from office is outrageously unfounded when compared to other cases of repeated and **flagrant** judicial misconduct which have resulted in no more than a public censure [reprimand]....[165]

But couples who have waited years and spent thousands to adopt saw the news as a **flagrant** example of a double standard that lets those with money dodge the usual requirements for adoption.[166]

write your own: |

Fledgling

'flej-li[ng]

(Adjective) inexperienced; beginner; little known
(Noun) a beginner; an inexperienced person
Keyword: sled team

The **fledgling sled team** from Jamaica made it to the Winter Olympics even though they had never seen snow.

The **fledgling** pilot dipped and zigzagged through the sky in an attempt to gain control of his plane.

But La Salle's vision far exceeded his ability. He overshot his mark by 400 miles. His ship, the Belle, foundered [became disabled] in a storm, and his **fledgling** settlement perished.[167]

Thomas Jefferson roughly doubled the size of the United States with the purchase of the Louisiana Territory from Napoleon Bonaparte. With the stroke of a pen, the **fledgling** U.S. took control of more than 830,000 square miles....[168]

write your own:

Foment

‘fO-”ment or fO-’ment

(Verb) to stir up or arouse
Keyword: foam

When the hottest teenage icon appeared wearing a **foam** outfit, a new fashion trend was **fomented** among teenagers.

The students were seated across the room from each other because they were sure to **foment** disturbances if they were together.

He knows how critical the fans in Philadelphia can be, how sports radio there can **foment** controversy...[169]

The powers in London, worried that Oglethorpe would **foment** war with Spain with his colonization and fortifications, asked him to withdraw from the coastal islands.[170]

write your own:

©Solid A, Inc. http://SolidA.net

Forestall

fOr-'stol or fo-'stol

(Verb) to avoid or delay (something)
Keyword: horse stall

The **horse stall** was so full of manure that Jerry **forestalled** cleaning it, finding other tasks to do.

The driver tried to **forestall** the accident by suddenly swerving to the shoulder of the road.

Wouldn't it be wonderful if we could always **forestall** problems by planning ahead?[171]

However, I am anxious to **forestall**, if possible, what appears to be a tragedy, the spectacle of a young man of your obvious mental gifts setting out deliberately to make a mess of his life.[172]

write your own: |

Fortuitous

for-'tü-&-t&s or f&r-'tyü-&-t&s

(Adjective) happening by a lucky chance
Keyword: fortune

The **fortuitous** man bet his lucky nickel in the slot machine and made a **fortune**.

Losing her job turned out to be a **fortuitous** event, as Jill discovered a better job the next day.

While no fine film was ever written without flashes of **fortuitous** inspiration, a screenplay is not an accident.[173]

In the southwest corner of the province, for example, Eastend (population 576) capitalized on the **fortuitous** discovery of some tyrannosaur bones (and later, some scientifically significant dinosaur poop) to attract a museum.[174]

write your own: |

128   ©Solid A, Inc.   http://SolidA.net

Gall

'gol

(Noun) brazen or rude boldness
Keyword: gall (bladder)

The doctor had a lot of **gall** to take out Joseph's **gall** bladder while removing his tonsils.

He was the only person who had the **gall** to stand up to our boss and say what we were all thinking.

[They] were all outsiders with the **gall** to challenge the incorrect assumptions held by the archaeologists of the day.[175]

Your new best friend Vivienne Upton had the **gall** to tell me at dinner that my entire life is predicated [based] on a despicable lie.[176]

write your own: |

(Verb) to store; to gather up and save
Keyword: gardener

The **gardener garnered** lots of strawberries to make enough jam for the rest of the year.

It has taken decades for my grandfather to **garner** thousands of coins for his antique collection.

Still, there may be comfort in knowing that even if you don't **garner** enough votes to win, your dress was in there pulling for you.[177]

As a senior partner in the firm he will **garner** a tremendous amount of respect and earn a very generous salary....[178]

write your own:

Garrulous

'gar-&-l&s or 'gar-y&-l&s

(Adjective) talkative, usually about unimportant things

Keyword: gargle

Garrulous Gus can't stop talking, even when he **gargles**.

At home Frank is laconic, but at work he is **garrulous**—rarely pausing for a second between words.

I'm pretty sure from his description that this inside man was the same guy I and a dozen other journalists interviewed.... It is unlikely that there was more than one **garrulous** Canadian advising the Haitian junta and talking to reporters.[179]

In the movies, your typical gangster is a fast-talking joker, a wisecrack machine brimming with raunchy, unprintable quips [clever remark]. In real life, though, mobsters tend to be a bit less **garrulous**.[180]

write your own: |

Gratuitous

gr&-'tü-&-t&s or gr&-'tyü-&-t&s

(Adjective) not required; uncalled for/
free or voluntary

Keyword: gut stew for us

On our exotic honeymoon our chef added a **gratuitous** bowl of **gut stew for us**, a local delicacy, which we had not ordered.

The film depicted **gratuitous** violence that was unnatural and forced into the script.

The empty shells of heavy [weaponry] lay everywhere, as did the twisted wrecks of cars, trucks, tanks, and APCs. The impression of vast, **gratuitous** destruction and carnage was only underlined and framed by the weirdly ordinary.[181]

His warts-and-all portraits include a few perhaps **gratuitous** details....[182]

write your own:

©Solid A, Inc.   http://SolidA.net

Guile

'gI&l or 'gIl

(Noun) trickery or deceit
Keyword: pile

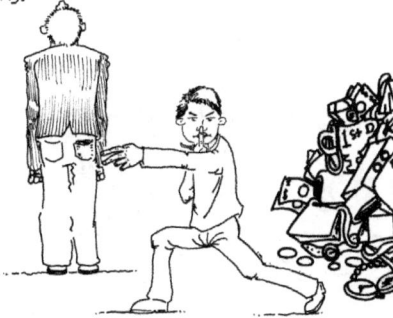

STAKE AT →
THIS
SPOT AND
WIN
A MILLION
DOLLARS!

The con artist used a lot of trickery and **guile** to produce a **pile** of loot.

Starving from hunger and malnutrition, the villagers relied on **guile** to swindle money and goods from the unsuspecting tourists.

Smith, 37, used his experience and **guile** to exploit the weaknesses of Buffalo's young receiver, Peerless Price, on a day when Bill's quarterback Drew Bledsoe threw 51 passes.[183]

Integrity also means avoiding any communication that is deceptive, full of **guile**, or beneath the dignity of people.[184]

write own:

Hackneyed

'hak-nEd

(Adjective) overused; without originality
Keyword: hacked in the knee

The hockey player was **hacked in the knee** so many times that his opponents' hits became **hackneyed**.

Duke used the word "cool" so often it has became **hackneyed** to his friends.

Is it hopelessly **hackneyed** even to suggest that an education is something to be coveted, then worked for, then cherished?[185]

In a completely different workshop, which she titles Intuitive Flower Painting, Stroud helps the students create spontaneous, fresh paintings of a **hackneyed** subject.[186]

write your own:

Hapless

'ha-pl&s

(Adjective) unlucky or unfortunate
Keyword: hatless

The **hapless** hat salesman became **hatless** after a strong wind blew all of his hats out to sea.

The **hapless** children looked longingly at the couple that entered the orphanage, hoping to be chosen for adoption.

[He] belongs to an elite arm of the state police ... whose job it is to bail out those **hapless** adventurers who find more excitement than they reckoned on.[187]

For generations, Lassie has been America's family pet. Braving fierce currents, rescuing victims from burning buildings, befriending **hapless** animals and humans alike—the intelligent and gentle collie quickly became every man's best friend.[188]

write your own:

'hOn

(Verb) to rub and sharpen/ to make something
perfect or more suitable
Keyword: bone

The cavemen **honed** their skills by sharpening their **bones** into arrows.

In preparation for Thanksgiving dinner, dad **honed** the carving knife to a perfect point.

[He] went back to school in 1990 to **hone** his photography skills and, after amassing so many credits, decided to get a degree.[189]

Since the middle of the nineteen thirties, the city's best sleight-of-hand [a cleverly executed trick] men have been getting together every Saturday afternoon at one restaurant or another to talk shop and **hone** the niceties [precision] of their craft.[190]

write your own: |

Hyperbole

hI-'p&r-b&-"lE   or   hI-'p&r-b&-lE

(Noun) extreme exaggeration
Keyword: hard to believe

Jim's **hyperboles** to describe the fish he caught were just too **hard to believe**.

Stories about Paul Bunyan and John Henry are full of **hyperboles** using extreme exaggerations.

On-camera, he speaks in **hyperbole**, makes every observation an exclamation, and constantly goes gaga over the people he profiles.[191]

I'm not certain of the real facts so I'll use **hyperbole** to get your attention.[192]

write your own:

(Adjective) not made up of matter/
not important
Keyword: material

Although the **material** in the emperor's new clothes was **immaterial** (not made up of matter), the emperor considered it **immaterial** (unimportant).

The fact that the team finally scored a goal was **immaterial**, as they still lost the game 6 to 1.

Whether or not they are founded in fact is completely **immaterial** to me, as I imagine it is to you as well; otherwise, you'd be reading Scientific American instead of this book.[193]

I will tell you another glory, brethren; sometimes when I meant to touch him I encountered a material, solid body; but at other times again when I felt him, his substance was **immaterial** and incorporeal [having no material body]... as if it did not exist at all.[194]

write your own: |

Impassive

im-'pa-siv

(Adjective) revealing no emotion
Keyword: pass

The **impassive** whistler did not act sympathetic toward those mourning at the funeral as he **passed**.

The **impassive** look on the defendant gave no indication that he was sentenced to life in prison.

The concern reaches the Capitol in ways both heart-wrenching and **impassive**, from the hand-written letter with a photo from the mother of a 10-year-old mentally disabled girl to the ready-made, anti-tax e-mails sent in bulk to every legislator.[195]

The director's orientation speech always begins the same way. The same words, met by the same **impassive** looks from his solemn, semi-detached audience.[196]

write your own: |

im-'p&r-vE-&s

(Adjective) impossible to penetrate or affect

Keyword: emperor

The **emperor** was **impervious** to any bad news, showing no emotion.

The author was very proud of his first book and was **impervious** to any negative criticism.

Animals that scavenged for a living would also have enjoyed an advantage. Lizards were, and are, largely **impervious** to the bacteria in rotting carcasses.[197]

The most rigid structures, the most **impervious** to change, will collapse first.[198]

write your own: |

Imprecation

"im-pri-'kA-sh&n

(Noun) a curse
Keyword: chimp vacation

The lab worker was angry and shouted all kinds of **imprecations** when he discovered that the lab had granted the monkeys a **chimp vacation**.

Because he chose to speak to his boss using **imprecations** when he was angry, he was suspended for one week without pay.

Outside court he enjoyed smoking cigars, quoting poetry, drinking claret … in Pomeroy's Wine Bar and muttering **imprecations** against his domineering wife.[199]

Harrison won't help clean up [the] mess he allegedly helped create in Graham's room. Shouts, screams, **imprecations**. "You're an idiot!" "Shut up!" "I hate you!"[200]

write **own:**
your

Section 5 Crossword Puzzle

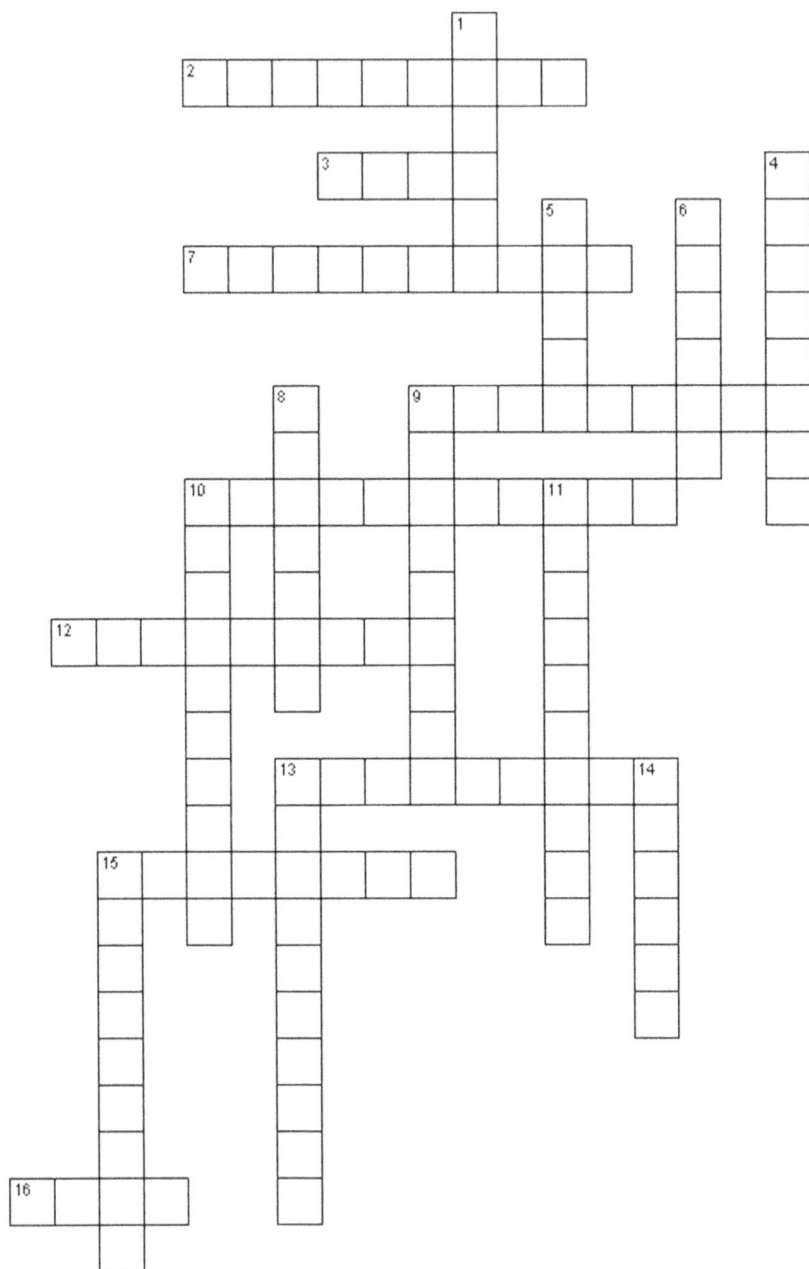

Across

2. talkative, usually about unimportant things

3. to rub and sharpen/ to make something perfect or more suitable

7. not required; uncalled for/ free or voluntary

9. extreme exaggeration

10. a curse

12. revealing no emotion

13. inexperienced; beginner; little known

15. scandalous, shocking, or outrageous

16. brazen or rude boldness

Down

1. to stir up or arouse

4. ineffective/ without care or responsibility

5. trickery or deceit

6. intense and sincere emotion

8. unlucky or unfortunate

9. overused; without originality

10. not made up of matter; not important

11. impossible to penetrate or affect

13. happening by a lucky chance

14. to store; to gather up and save

15. to avoid or delay (something)

Section 5 Matching Review

Fill in the blank with the best answer.

1. Linda did not appreciate the _____ her teenage daughter used when she was with her friends.
    a. imprecations   b. hyperboles   c. fervor   d. gall

2. Due to Jill's _____ for selling real estate, she sold more houses than anyone else in the state.
    a. gall   b. fervor   c. imprecation   d. guile

3. The teacher attempted to _____ any bad behavior in the class-room by over-planning her activities for the day.
    a. garner   b. forestall   c. hackney   d. foment

4. Though Joan sat down to do her homework, her _____ and lackadaisical approach left her unable to complete the assignment on time.
    a. feckless   b. gratuitous   c. immaterial   d. flagrant

5. Since losing much of his money at the casino and on the stock mar-ket, Bill has become a(n) _____, and somewhat solitary, man.
    a. garrulous   b. hapless   c. gratuitous   d. gratuitous

6. Jean, a fledgling actor, met the Hollywood director in a(n) _____ car accident in which no one was hurt and resulted in a leading role for Jean in the director's movie.
    a. gratuitous   b. hapless   c. fortuitous   d. hapless

7. My neighbor had the _____ to make insulting remarks about the flowers in my backyard.
    a. fervor   b. guile   c. imprecation   d. gall

8. I was worried when the grape juice spilled on the new table, but luckily, the tablecloth was _____ to liquid and nothing soaked through.
    a. hapless   b. impervious   c. impassive   d. immaterial

9. It took a long time hiking in the woods to _____ enough wild mushrooms for dinner.
    a. garner   b. hone   c. forestall   d. foment

10. Even the reporters were unable to get a word in as the _____ speaker spoke rapidly without taking a breath.
a. hapless   b. garrulous   c. gratuitous   d. hapless

11. The televised surgery captured all of the _____ details, including close-ups of the incisions, blood and guts.
a. flagrant   b. impervious   c. gratuitous   d. feckless

12. The stirring picture was shown only for a minute on the news because it _____ such a strong emotion from the audience.
a. fomented   b. honed   c. hackneyed   d. forestalled

13. His _____ poker face was not readable, making him a champion card player.
a. fortuitous   b. garrulous   c. impassive   d. impervious

14. Ruth Ann was considered to be trustworthy, lacking any _____.
a. gall   b. hyperbole   c. fervor   d. guile

15. Although emotionally moving, the movie becomes quickly _____ when viewed more than once.
a. hackneyed   b. immaterial   c. feckless   d. fledgling

16. Frank enrolled in the advanced glass blowing course in order to _____ his glass blowing techniques.
a. garner   b. foment   c. hone   d. forestall

17. Uncertain of the real facts about her family history, Gale embellished her family story with _____.
a. imprecations   b. foment   c. guile   d. hyperboles

18. New to the game of soccer, the _____ soccer player accidentally scored a point for the other team.
a. forestalled   b. honed   c. hackneyed   d. fledgling

19. Having a perfect score on the final test was _____ because her average for the class was still well below a passing grade.
a. fledgling   b. impassive   c. hackneyed   d. immaterial

20. The referee kicked the basketball player out of the game after the _____ foul.
a. impassive   b. fledgling   c. flagrant   d. garrulous

Section 5 Matching Review

Match the word on the left to the correct meaning on the right.

1. _____ Feckless
2. _____ Fervor
3. _____ Flagrant
4. _____ Fledgling
5. _____ Foment
6. _____ Forestall
7. _____ Fortuitous
8. _____ Gall
9. _____ Garner
10. _____ Garrulous
11. _____ Gratuitous
12. _____ Guile
13. _____ Hackneyed
14. _____ Hapless
15. _____ Hone
16. _____ Hyperbole
17. _____ Immaterial
18. _____ Impassive
19. _____ Impervious
20. _____ Imprecation

A. to stir up or arouse
B. impossible to penetrate or affect
C. not made up of matter; not important
D. to rub and sharpen/ to make something perfect or more suitable
E. happening by a lucky chance
F. overused; without originality
G. talkative, usually about unimportant things
H. brazen or rude boldness
I. not required; uncalled for/ free or voluntary
J. scandalous, shocking, or outrageous
K. trickery or deceit
L. ineffective/ without care or responsibility
M. intense and sincere emotion
N. a curse
O. extreme exaggeration
P. to store; to gather up and save
Q. to avoid or delay (something)
R. unlucky or unfortunate
S. inexperienced; beginner; little known
T. revealing no emotion

Section Six

Inadvertent

"i-n&d-'v&r-t&nt

(Adjective) unintentional; careless
Keyword: in advertisement

The BMW president was furious about the **inadvertent** mistake **in the advertisement** stating that the latest model could be purchased for one hundred dollars.

Chris's **inadvertent** wrong turn accidentally landed him in rush hour traffic.

Consider tape-recording your interviews with police personnel. You want to ensure that your thoughts are not **inadvertently** misconstrued, misparaphrased, or overly abbreviated.[201]

Of immediate concern is whether technical glitches, **inadvertent** errors or confusion over the regulations would jeopardize universities or foreign students.[202]

write your own: |

Inane

i-'nAn

(Adjective) foolish or silly; lacking significance
Keyword: insane

The **inane** class clown was acting **insane** by standing on his head on the seat of his chair.

Bringing zoo animals to the birthday party was an **inane** idea as the animals ruined the expensive carpets and furniture.

That's just ridiculous. No reputable producer would ever do a show based on such an **inane** concept.[203]

Dreamcatcher is a moviegoer's nightmare. The story is incoherent [disorderly and confusing], **inane** and interminable [seemingly endless].[204]

write your own:

Indefatigable

"in-di-'fa-ti-g&-b&l

(Adjective) incapable of being tired
Keyword: in the fatigues

When he's **in the fatigues**, he is **indefatigable**--able to outlast all of the other soldiers during the drills.

Never giving up, he's been **indefatigable** in his quest to find a cure for cancer.

It soon became apparent that this schedule, even for the **indefatigable** Dr. Morton, was too demanding.[205]

The conquest of majestic Mount Everest caught the imagination of the world, bringing an unprecedented number of climbers each spring and fall. It also brought the Sherpas a generous and **indefatigable** benefactor [someone who does good to others] in the person of [Sir Edmund] Hillary.[206]

write your own: |

                http://SolidA.net

Indolent

'in-d&-l&nt

(Adjective) habitually lazy or idle
Keyword: spindle bent

The **spindle bent** when the **indolent** movers dropped it down the stairs because they were too lazy to carry it.

Alex's **indolent** work habits led to very poor grades when he went to college.

Just as the **indolent** were not reprimanded [reproved or scolded], the best and the brightest—the teachers and principals who labored heroically against the odds—were neither rewarded nor commended [praised].[207]

The novelist ... reckons our obsession with sportswear is "an indication of the progressively more **indolent,** lazy, couch potato mentality of the great mass of people."[208]

write your own:

Ingenuous

in-'jen-y&-w&s

(Adjective) displaying openness and simplicity often in a childlike manner; frank; naïve; trusting

Keyword: genuine

The jeweler spoke **ingenuously** about the **genuine** gems in the jewelry store, pointing out all the cracks and imperfections to his customers.

Margaret's friends had to watch out for her when they went places. She was so **ingenuous** they were afraid that someone would try to take advantage of her.

How unsuspecting, how **ingenuous** I've been. For weeks now I've been the dupe [fooled by] of a conspiracy.[209]

Human beings can build a magnificent reality in adulthood out of what was only an illusion in early childhood—their loving, joyous, trusting, **ingenuous**, unrealistic over idealization of their two parents.[210]

write your own: |

Insipid

in-'si-p&d

(Adjective) tasteless/ dull; lacking interest or spirit
Keyword: sip

A **sip** of the **insipid** cola instantly told her that it had been opened several days ago, and had lost most of its fizz and flavor.

Thanksgiving dinner at Aunt Joyce's was rather **insipid**. The wine was flat, the turkey like cardboard, and the sauce quite tasteless.

Alex was a Catholic boy. He had been taught plenty about hell. But the searing realities of the [prison camps] in which he spent most of his twenties would soon make all that pulpit hellfire seem **insipid**.[211]

When they open the door of cell 111 and shove me in, the soup is sitting there on my plate, cold ... I will have to eat it right away, cold and **insipid** as it is....[212]

write your own:

in-'säl-v&nt or "in-'sol-v&nt

(Adjective) unable to pay debts; bankrupt
Keyword: solve

Unable to **solve** any mysteries the detective became **insolvent** and had to close his office.

The couple declared bankruptcy after finding out from their accountant they were **insolvent**.

Recently more than one hundred of America's wealthiest men and women who invested in the prestigious but now **insolvent** insurance company, Lloyd's of London, lost all their personal assets when their promissory notes to pay off Lloyd's debts were called in on a moment's notice.[213]

State legislators are expected to put the finishing touches today on a bill to provide an emergency $100-million state loan for the **insolvent** school district....[214]

write your own:

Intractable

in-'trak-t&-b&l or "in-'trak-t&-

(Adjective) not easily managed or manipulated
Keyword: tractor

The **intractable tractor** refused to be operated by the farmer.

Romeo and Juliet could not solve the **intractable** problems between their families.

Find a cheap, renewable and clean form of energy ... [and many of the world's problems would] be solved. Yet [without] energy, many global problems remain **intractable**.[215]

It would be easy to conclude that cement is a rotten business and accept high costs, slow growth, and customer dissatisfaction ... But starting in the early 1990s, new leadership realized that solving these seemingly **intractable** problems would give [them] a unique position in the industry.[216]

write your own:

Intrepid

in-'tre-p&d

(Adjective) fearless or adventurous
Keyword: in trap

The **intrepid** explorer caught a fierce polar bear **in a trap**.

The **intrepid** rock climber constantly searched for more challenging places to climb.

So when it was put to him that there might be scientific and political value in sending a party to explore the interior of America beyond the Mississippi he leapt at the idea, hoping the **intrepid** adventurers would find herds of healthy mastodons ... grazing on the bounteous plains. [regarding Lewis and Clark's famous expedition][217]

On May 29, 1953, at 11: 30 on a blustery morning, the two **intrepid** souls [Sir Edmund Hillary and Tenzing Norgay] stood side by side, about 29,000 feet above sea level [on Mt. Everest].[218]

write your own: |

Inure

i-'nur or i-'nyur

(Verb) to become used to something unpleasant;
to harden
Keyword: a lure

The lousy fisherman got **a lure** caught in his back so many times he became **inured** to the painful process of having it removed.

After serving years in the prison cell, the prisoner became **inured** to hardships.

War Admiral [a racing horse] was a raging lion behind the gate, and Smith was concerned that Seabiscuit would take one look at his opponent's tantrum and throw one of his own. He needed to expose Seabiscuit to a similarly unruly gate horse and **inure** him to the sight of it.[219]

Its purpose, much like the physical beatings, is to **inure** the senses to insult [hardship], to harden the will against responding with rage and fear....[220]

write your own: |

Irascible

i-'ra-s&-b&l

(Adjective) easily provoked or angered

Keyword: harass

Due to Jane's quick temper and **irascible** nature, students thought it was funny to **harass** her.

As Cindy's daughter grew into a teenager, she became more volatile and **irascible** than ever.

He rarely gives interviews, but when he does, he's about the bluntest, most **irascible**, most straight-talkin' guy out there.[221]

Unusually clever for a white dragon, [he] has a personality like an icy, rusted blade. He is **irascible**, unpleasant, and thoroughly evil. [222]

write your own:

     http://SolidA.net

Judicious

ju-'di-sh&s

(Adjective) having or showing reason
and good judgment
Keyword: judge

The **judicious judge** was so fair that after he made a decision in a case everyone was happy.

The teacher's **judicious** use of praise and discipline encouraged the students to work harder and perform better.[223]

Edelman is so **judicious** and fair-minded, he seems born to be a judge.

And Microsoft has approached the Xbox hardware with a software mentality—emphasizing a laundry list of marketable features over **judicious**, timely design. [224]

write your own: |

Lachrymose

'la-kr&-"mOs

(Adjective) sad; given easily to tears
Keyword: lack the most

The child that **lacked the most** toys was **lachrymose** and began to cry.

The **lachrymose** puppy whined and cried every time its owners left it alone.

Referring to his involuntary retirement in 1964, he claimed the manner of his going as a proud achievement. He was not referring to his **lachrymose** farewell speech at the party... that gave him his marching orders [orders to leave or move on].[225]

Canadian Counter-tenor Matthew White "reclaims" the work here to open his excellent recital of elegiac [sorrowful], **lachrymose** music from the 17th and 18th Centuries.[226]

write own:

Lassitude

‘la-s&-”tüd or ‘la-s&-”tyüd

(Noun) physical or mental weariness; sluggishness
Keyword: lasso dude

While performing in the rodeo, **Lasso Dude** was overcome by a feeling of **lassitude** and was unable to finish his performance.

After completing the marathon, a feeling of **lassitude** overcame the runners.

If one word sums up a constellation of reactions in a myriad of towns, villages and cities at the end of the war, it is **lassitude**. Exhaustion was the prevailing feeling after four-and-a-half years of carnage [destruction].[227]

The first Matrix [a movie] succeeded in making alienation captivating: It proposed that the everyday world of the late 20th century was the creation of conquering machines that numbed humans into **lassitude**, then fed off their bioelectrical force.[228]

write your own:

'll-&-"nIz

(Verb) to treat as a celebrity
Keyword: lion

The **lion** was **lionized** after playing the lead role in the most popular movie in the jungle and was treated like a celebrity.

At the piano recital, the young girl was **lionized** for her exceptional performance. One small child even asked for her autograph.

Canadian photographers lined up to **lionize** Yousuf Karsh last night as the eminent [famous] Canadian portrait shooter [photographer].[229]

While journalists **lionize** the goal scorer ... "coaches must find ways to break down this traditional and simple analysis"—often by highlighting the less eye-catching lead-up work of teammates.[230]

write your own: |

Loquacious

lO-'kwA-sh&s

(Adjective) talking excessively
Keyword: locust

The **loquacious locust** talked so much that the other bugs stopped listening.

The **loquacious** professor rarely allowed his students to ask a question, let alone get a word in edgewise.

The **loquacious** private shareholder known for taking the microphone at annual meetings with a string of questions ranging from the political to the pedantic [academic], is moving into top gear.[231]

Still, the many clips transport us to the time when Paar personified must-see TV on NBC, with his rambling, personal monologues [a one-person show] as well as free-flowing conversation that proved the **loquacious** host was also a superior listener.[232]

write your own: _____

_____

Lugubrious

lu-'gü-brE-&s or lu-'gyü-brE-&s

(Adjective) mournful or very sad/ dismal
Keyword: love glue

Cherie felt **lugubrious** when all of her friends received a dose of **love glue** from cupid, but she was somehow overlooked.

The child was **lugubrious** after her puppy ran away from home and nothing could console her.

I saw tears on the faces of many former Rebels. Even Mrs. Shau looked **lugubrious**. They had a mask for every occasion.[233]

There they stood as the [hockey] game ended, with Tikkanen wearing his trademark manic grin, Gretzky the **lugubrious** look of an unwilling dance partner.[234]

write your own: |

Maladroit

"ma-l&-'droit

(Adjective) clumsy or bumbling; awkward
Keyword: mail android (as in a robot that delivers mail)

The **maladroit mail android** was so clumsy he was unable to get the mail into the mailboxes.

The **maladroit** cowboy made a hilarious rodeo clown where his clumsy and awkward nature was a natural fit for the job.

My sister asked me to review a video game for her 8-year-old son, something she can't do herself, because she's technologically **maladroit**....[235]

[He] can give a dynamite presentation to a big audience, but seems awkward in groups and **maladroit** at small talk.[236]

write your own:

(Verb) to spoil or damage
Keyword: Mars

With the meteorite showers, **Mars** became very **marred**.

The figure skater's performance was **marred** by a stumble during a double axel spin attempt.

Flocks of tourists laden with cameras perch on a bluff opposite the town to capture on film the magic moment when the setting sun turns the town to gold. Their shots are **marred**, however, because the house in their immediate foreground has collapsed in an untidy heap of mud, like a sand castle overcome by the tide.[237]

He had stern, handsome features **marred** only when his upper lip lifted to reveal a set of yellow [horse like] teeth.[238]

write your own: |

Meager

'mE-g&r

(Adjective) inadequate; lacking in quality or number
Keyword: Me, girl.

Jane's clothes were quite **meager** when she met her Tuxedo Tarzan. Upon their meeting, Jane announced, "**Me, girl.**"

She could not afford a new CD on her **meager** allowance.

Back in port—with their nets, buoys and lobster traps ruined by oil—their **meager** catch was rejected by the health authorities.[239]

Everyone took wood back to camp to eke out the **meager** fuel ration we were allowed for the barracks stove, and the guards always demanded that twenty-five per cent of what we brought back be turned over to them for their private use.[240]

write your own:

Section 6 Crossword Puzzle

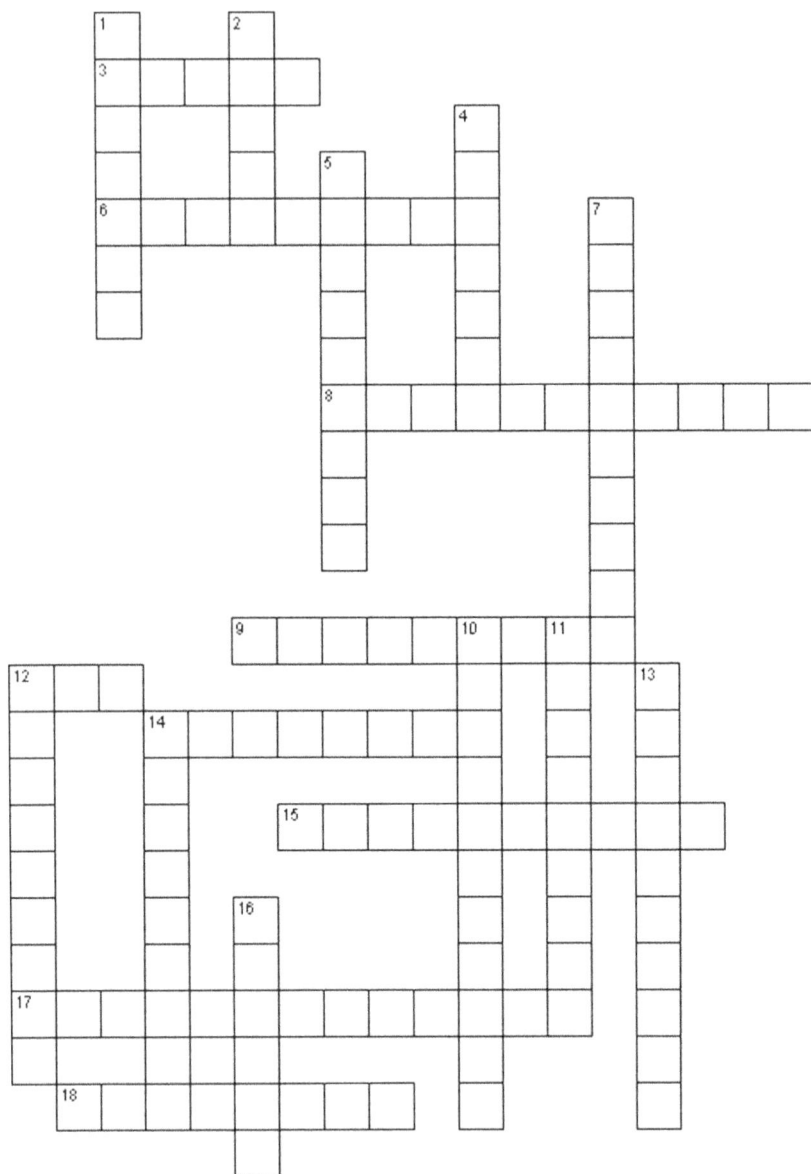

Across

3. foolish or silly; lacking significance

6. displaying openness and simplicity often in a childlike manner; frank; naïve; trusting

8. unintentional; careless

9. easily provoked or angered

12. to spoil or damage

14. habitually lazy or idle

15. talking excessively

17. incapable of being tired

18. fearless or adventurous

Down

1. to treat as a celebrity

2. to become used to something unpleasant; to harden

4. tasteless/ dull; lacking interest or spirit

5. having or showing reason and good judgment

7. sad; given easily to tears

10. not easily managed or manipulated

11. physical or mental weariness; sluggishness

12. clumsy or bumbling; awkward

13. mournful; very sad

14. unable to pay debts; bankrupt

16. inadequate; lacking in quality or number

Section 6 Multiple Choice Review

Fill in the blank with the best answer.

1. Part of the downfall of the economy is due to people losing their jobs, making them _____ as consumers.
   a. insolvent   b. intrepid   c. indefatigable   d. intractable

2. Ken was a(n) _____ tennis player. Not only was he clumsy, he also hit most of the tennis balls over the fence.
   a. maladroit   b. meager   c. lachrymose   d. judicious

3. Roger's boss fired him for his _____ attitude toward work when he caught Roger sitting down on the job again.
   a. intrepid   b. judicious   c. ingenuous   d. indolent

4. The movie was so sad that the audience left the theater feeling _____ .
   a. inane   b. marred   c. indefatigable   d. lugubrious

5. The telemarketer was _____ to constant rejection and was able to ignore rude people.
   a. marred   b. inured   c. lionized   d. indolent

6. Vince's music was so _____ that it bored his entire audience within minutes.
   a. maladroit   b. insipid   c. lassitude   d. indolent

7. Tragically the military _____ shot down their own plane during a military exercise.
   a. insipidly   b. inadvertently   c. intractably   d. irascibly

8. The secret to mom's great potato salad recipe is a(n) _____ amount of mayonnaise with a couple tablespoons of German mustard.
   a. inadvert   b. ingenuous   c. judicious   d. insipid

9. _____ conflicts, like the feud between the Hatfields and McCoys, often take generations to solve.
   a. lugubrious   b. insolvent   c. insipid   d. intractable

10. A(n) _____ 20 fans attended the championship match in the huge dome stadium.
    a. inane   b. intrepid   c. inadvertent   d. meager

11. The prisoner was so moody and _____ that the guards were afraid to speak to him.
    a. irascible   b. judicious   c. insipid   d. intractable

12. Susan is so _____ that nearly anything will set her off crying.
    a. loquacious   b. irascible   c. lachrymose   d. lassitude

13. After studying for the test for many hours, Paul felt a great sense of _____ and wanted to get some rest.
    a. lionization   b. lassitude   c. judiciousness   d. lugubriousness

14. Cameron was _____ as the local hero after rescuing a child from a burning building.
    a. inured   b. marred   c. inane   d. lionized

15. The hairdresser is very _____; she talks non-stop to her customers for hours.
    a. lugubrious   b. inane   c. lachrymose   d. loquacious

16. Seven years after leaving the orphanage, the _____ search for her twin sister paid off.
    a. indolent   b. inadvertent   c. indefatigable   d. insolvent

17. His near perfect report card was _____ by one "D."
    a. inured   b. marred   c. lionized   d. insolvent

18. Because he appeared too naïve and trusting, the _____ young man was mugged in the subway.
    a. loquacious   b. indefatigable   c. ingenuous   d. meager

19. The _____ firefighters remained calm as the fire unexpectedly flared up and changed direction.
    a. intrepid   b. insipid   c. maladroit   d. irascible

20. Many of Josh's friends fail to take him seriously due to his _____ sense of humor.
    a. irascible   b. lachrymose   c. inured   d. inane

Section 6 Matching Review

Match the word on the left to the correct meaning on the right.

1. _____ Inadvertent

2. _____ Inane

3. _____ Indefatigable

4. _____ Indolent

5. _____ Ingenuous

6. _____ Insipid

7. _____ Insolvent

8. _____ Intractable

9. _____ Intrepid

10. _____ Inure

11. _____ Irascible

12. _____ Judicious

13. _____ Lachrymose

14. _____ Lassitude

15. _____ Lionize

16. _____ Loquacious

17. _____ Lugubrious

18. _____ Maladroit

19. _____ Mar

20. _____ Meager

A. displaying openness and simplicity often in a childlike manner; frank; naïve; trusting

B. having or showing reason and good judgment

C. unintentional; careless

D. sad; given easily to tears

E. tasteless/ dull; lacking interest or spirit

F. mournful or very sad

G. habitually lazy or idle

H. not easily managed or manipulated

I. to become used to something unpleasant; to harden

J. physical or mental weariness; sluggishness

K. talking excessively

L. to spoil or damage

M. incapable of being tired

N. unable to pay debts; bankrupt

O. fearless or adventurous

P. easily provoked or angered

Q. to treat as a celebrity

R. foolish or silly; lacking significance

S. clumsy or bumbling; awkward

T. inadequate; lacking in quality or number

Section Seven

Mendicant

'men-di-k&nt

(Noun) a beggar
Keyword: mending can

THANKS

She gave out **mending cans** to all the **mendicants** on the street, hoping they would sew the holes in their clothes.

The volunteers worked like **mendicants**, begging strangers for donations for the new church.

While there are no laws against begging in Jerusalem, the police and the municipality continue to be at loggerheads [quarrelsome disagreement] over which of their departments is responsible for regulating the **mendicants'** activities.[241]

For [former United Kingdom Prime Minister] Churchill's part there was the detestation [extreme dislike] that is often felt by the **mendicant**; he hated having to be polite to the man he was asking for a loan.[242]

write your own:

Morose

m&-'rOs or mo-'rOs

(Adjective) gloomy; expressing sadness
Keyword: more roses

Spending his first birthday alone, he sent himself even **more roses** to help alleviate his **morose** feelings.

Instead of feeling excited at her high school graduation, Christy felt **morose** at the prospect of starting college in a new town.

Teammates tried again to pull Contreras out of his funk [state of depression]. They asked him out to dinner, asked him to play cards. But he declined, and faced another **morose** night alone, thinking about his wife and children back in Cuba.[243]

Colorado artists, both those obsessed with **morose** black-and-white photography, as well as watercolor traditionalists, make a strong showing this Memorial Day weekend.[244]

write your own:

"m&l-t&-'far-E-&s

(Adjective) characterized by great variety or diversity
Keyword: multiple Ferris Wheels

Multiple Ferris Wheels of all shapes and sizes became a **multifarious** attraction at the fair.

The convention drew a **multifarious** crowd with diverse occupations and backgrounds.

The world's top club competition, the Club Cup brings together the best teams from the **multifarious** leagues in Europe....[245]

In his famous essay ... the poet suggests that the "monotony of the Dutch landscape gave rise to dreams of **multifarious**, colorful, and unusual flora [vegetation]."[246]

write your own:

Nadir

'nA-d&r or 'nA-"dir

(Noun) worst moment; the lowest point
Keyword: gator

The **gator** reached his **nadir** when he was caught and transported to the zoo.

The **nadir** of my life was the day my car was wrecked, my girlfriend broke up with me, and I tripped and broke my leg.

The 2002 election marked the modern **nadir** of the Democratic Party in Colorado. Republicans wrestled the state Senate from the Democrats, retained control of the House and re-elected Bill Owens governor.[247]

The glory was a long time coming for the Dayton Flyers, a proud basketball program that had gone 17-67 in a three-season **nadir** from 1992 to 1995.[248]

write your own:

'ne-gli-j&-b&l

(Adjective) unimportant; not worth considering
Keyword: vegetable

After the severe drought this summer our **vegetable** crop was **negligible** compared to previous years.

New radon detectors can detect even a **negligible** amount of radon so homes can be kept safe.

They wanted to start a flag football team, but the Hernando High athletic director could not oblige, even though the overhead for the sport would be **negligible**.[249]

Officials at the Auto Club of Southern California have predicted only a slight drop in the number of Southern Californians flying or driving this weekend, and said it might even be **negligible**.[250]

write **own:**
your

Obscure

äb-'skyur or &b-'skyur

(Adjective) not well known/
unclear; difficult to understand
Keyword: Oz's cure (as in Wizard of Oz)

No one understood **Oz's cure** for the Tin Man as it was very **obscure**.

No one completely understood the book's **obscure** reference to the hidden treasure.

The traces of half-**obscure** scratching combined with cracks running through the masonry made patterns that my mind naturally reshaped into concrete images....[251]

In 1984, as a largely **obscure** three-term New York representative, [Geraldine Ferraro] joined the Democratic ticket with Walter Mondale, becoming the first woman ever nominated by a major party for Vice President.[252]

write own:

Obstreperous

&b-'stre-p&-r&s or äb-'stre-pr&s

(Adjective) noisy and difficult to deal with; defiant

Keyword: step on us

Their last words were, "Don't **step on us**," but the **obstreperous** monster was defiant and refused to obey.

The waitress decided to give the incoming party a table in the back of the restaurant because she knew they had a tendency to be noisy and **obstreperous**.

In the midst of the week-long debate, Lawrence, who had been on his best behavior, began to revert to his old ways. When, becoming **obstreperous**, he made an impudent [sassy] remark, no one knew what to say.[253]

Now suppose there are parents who are **obstreperous**, cranky, and argumentative, who insist on running the household and refuse to hand over anything....[254]

write your own:

                    http://SolidA.net

Officious

(Adjective) eager to give advice or services when
they are not wanted; meddlesome
Keyword: official

The **officious official** kept interfering in the basketball game
to give the players advice.

The teenage girl felt that her parents were rather **officious**
when they read her diary and listened to her phone conversations.

They defied the **officious** ushers who tried to keep them in
their cushioned seats, erupting at the slightest shout or hip
twitch from the minister of the New Super Heavy Funk.[255]

A veritable [authentic] army of auctioneers from the National Auction Group of Gadsden, Alabama, all wearing
matching American-flag ties, were doing their **officious** best
to prod, prod, prod.[256]

write your own: |

Opulent

'ä-py&-l&nt

(Adjective) rich or wealthy

Keyword: opal

The **opulent** movie star showed off her wealth by wearing lots of **opal** jewels.

The **opulent** hotel was decorated with lots of fresh flowers, luxurious fabrics, and dark, rich paint to create a grand feeling for the customers.

Air Force families had fond memories of a charming country peopled by strange yet amiable [friendly] folk, affording an **opulent** lifestyle replete with luxurious homes, servants, and nannies....[257]

Neither side is immoral, unless their values get pushed to an excess of **opulent** indulgence on one hand or miserly bargain-driving on the other.[258]

write your own:

Pallid

'pa-l&d

(Adjective) lacking color or liveliness
Keyword: salad

The week-old **salad** looked **pallid** and lifeless.

Henry could tell that his wife was not feeling well because of her **pallid** color.

She imagines Caddie's shoulders swelling up out of an evening gown, smooth and flawless and peachy, and compares this rose-tinted vision with her own **pallid** torso, whose collar-bones jut out from her freckled chest like the handles of a grid-iron.[259]

The 33-year-old breast-cancer patient's cheeks had turned **pallid**, her skin "dry, ashen and leathery"....[260]

write your own: |

Paradigm

'par-&-"dIm or 'par-&-"dim

(Noun) a model or example/a way of thinking
Keyword: pair of dimes

The introduction of the **pair of dimes** to the natives began a new **paradigm** for their trading.

Copernicus developed a new astronomical **paradigm** describing how the earth and other planets move around the sun.

Technologists, like scientists, tend to hold on to their theories until incontrovertible [not able to refute] evidence, usually in the form of failures, convinces them to accept new **paradigms**.[261]

Zizek does clever things with the paradoxes [contradictions] inherent in this situation, but in the end he is reduced to arguing that people don't need another **paradigm**; they just need to act, to break out of the box of received ideas, and meaning will take care of itself.[262]

write your own: |

Pariah

p&-'rI-&

(Noun) an outcast
Keyword: parade

The **pariah** was **paraded** through the streets on his way to jail.

When the spy was discovered selling secrets, he became a **pariah** in the eyes of his country.

The boys there have ostracized [excluded] him for his vanity and self-absorption, and he is a **pariah**.[263]

He won his seat in 1992 by unseating a well-liked incumbent [an official who holds an office] who was the GOP [Grand Old Party - Republicans] caucus' only woman, and the following year became a **pariah** after breaking with every Republican colleague by voting against a spending plan that raised taxes.[264]

write own:
your

'pär-t&-z&n or 'pär-t&-san

(Noun) a loyal supporter
(Adjective) devoted
Keyword: party

The **partisans** had a **party** to show their support for the Democratic President.

The speaker was careful not to take a **partisan** line when he told stories about both political parties in the Presidential debates.

They each behaved at times as if the world is now safe for us to be both insular [narrow viewpoint] and mindlessly **partisan** on every issue.[265]

John ... stressed the importance of a bipartisan [two political party] approach: "Part of our challenge today is how do we become more political and not become more **partisan**."[266]

write your **own**:

Pellucid

p&-'lü-s&d

(Adjective) transparent; clear
Keyword: polluted

Over time the transparent water in the **pellucid** lake became **polluted** and murky.

After the window was cleaned, it was once again **pellucid** and helped to brighten the room.

The desert storm is over and through the pure sweet **pellucid** air the cliff swallows and the nighthawks plunge and swerve, making cries of hunger and warning....[267]

Downstream, [they] found themselves in a midday rise, trout leaving the stream bed—every spot and speckle visible in the **pellucid** water and bright sunlight—to intercept mayflies hatching out on the surface.[268]

write your own: |

p&r-'fi-dE-&s or "p&r-'fi-dE-&s

(Adjective) treacherous; not trustworthy
Keyword: hideous

The **perfidious** villain had a **hideous** face that could not be trusted.

The zoo caretakers had to be careful, especially when feeding the tigers. They were considered **perfidious** and extremely dangerous when hungry.

According to his ex-wife ... 50 years after their marriage, he was rude and **perfidious**.[269]

When our nation is at war with any other, we detest them under the character of cruel, **perfidious**, unjust and violent: But always esteem ourselves and allies equitable, moderate, and merciful.[270]

write your own: |

Permeable

'p&r-mE-&-b&l

(Adjective) having small holes allowing substances to pass through; penetrable
Keyword: perming a bull

When **perming a bull**, make sure to use rollers that are **permeable** to allow the air to penetrate to give it that soft full curl.

Coffee filters are **permeable** and allow coffee to flow through them, but not the coffee grounds.

Passing a small, direct electric current through the skin can make the epidermis **permeable** to many other drugs—including proteins.[271]

For most of us, most of the time, language is not a big issue. It's just there, like skin—a delicate, **permeable** membrane that supplies an essential barrier between our vulnerable emotions and the outside world.[272]

write own:

"p&r-sp&-'kA-sh&s

(Adjective) keen at perceiving and understanding;
sharp witted
Keyword: perspiration

Although Shaq offered to wash his jersey before giving it away, the **perspicacious** fan knew it was worth more with Shaq's **perspiration**.

Jason had a **perspicacious** capability for solving puzzles and riddles, no matter how difficult.

In exploring the showdown between [Fomer United Kingdom Prime Mister] Churchill and Hitler ... [he] presents Churchill consistently as the more **perspicacious** statesman.[273]

It would also be interesting to see if he was really as **perspicacious** as they said he was.[274]

write your own: |

Petulant

'pe-ch&-l&nt

(Adjective) bad tempered; rude or impatient; irritable
Keyword: pet for rent

The **petulant pet for rent** bared its teeth and growled before chewing up the man's leg.

The customer's **petulant** behavior was rude and difficult to deal with.

She was being what my father called "petulant," as in, "Susie, don't speak to me in that **petulant** tone."[275]

Most parents shake their heads and blame hormones when their teenager storms off and slams the door. But new research suggests that such **petulant** behavior could actually be due to normal brain "remodeling" that occurs during adolescence.[276]

write own: _____

Philanthropic

"fi-l&n-'thrä-pik

(Adjective) being charitable or generous
Keyword: Phil in the tropics

Phil in the Tropics was a **philanthropic** hero, providing generous help to anyone in need.

The **philanthropic** businessman used his wealth to help the poor in his community.

His strong views on these subjects clearly influenced his five children. Assorted do-gooders, they're all involved in their father's **philanthropic** endeavors.[277]

Al Green ... was recently appointed to the Order of Canada in recognition of life-long **philanthropic** activities.[278]

write your own:

Phlegmatic

fleg-'ma-tik

(Adjective) unemotional; sluggish; dull
Keyword: flag mat

Because they felt it was not right to step on a flag mat, the **phlegmatic** employees worked especially slow to fill their orders for **flag mats**.

The **phlegmatic** psychologist had the ideal personality for his job because he had no trouble keeping emotional distance from his clients.

[He] was a **phlegmatic** man, a college graduate ... with an easy manner that the [Chicago's baseball team] Cubs interpreted as a lack of spirit.[279]

One realized the red-hot energy which underlay [Sherlock] Holmes's **phlegmatic** exterior when one saw the sudden change which came over him from the moment that he entered the fatal apartment. In an instant he was tense and alert....[280]

write your own: |

Section 7 Crossword Puzzle

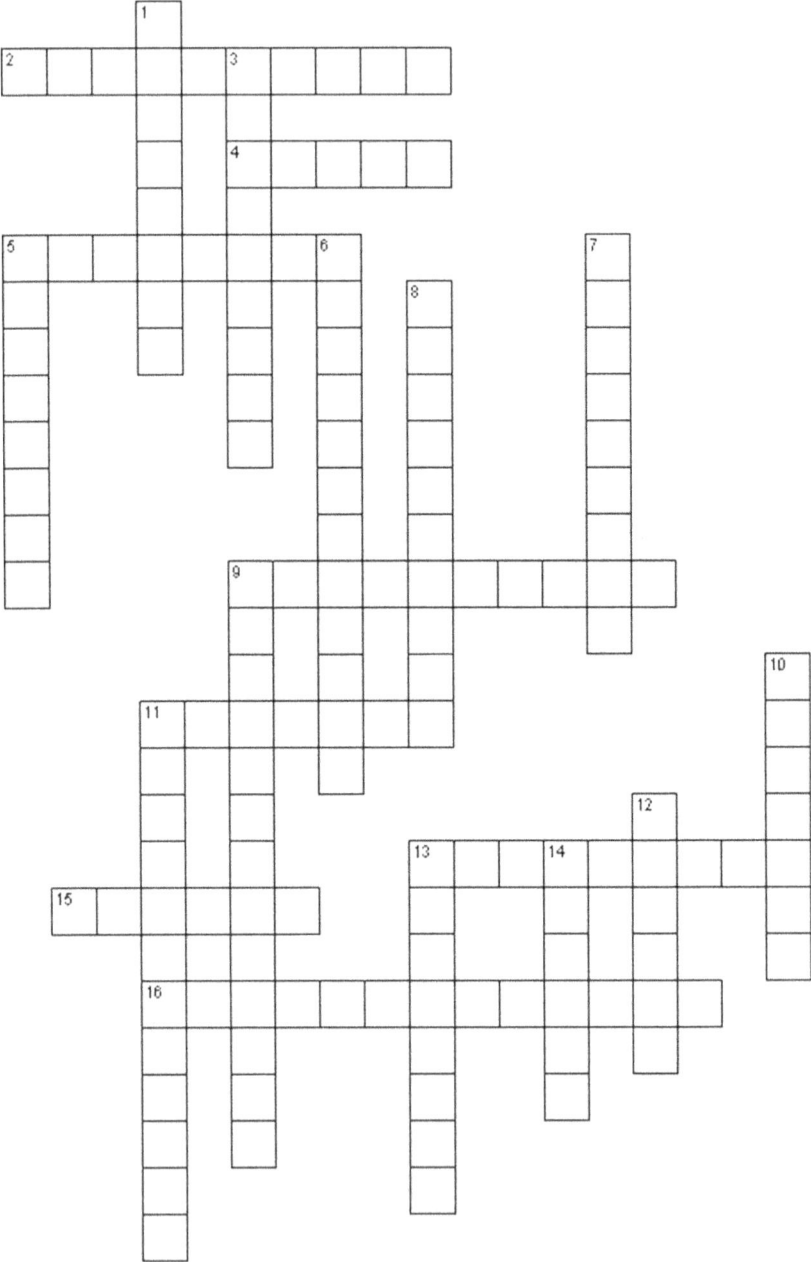

©Solid A, Inc.   http://SolidA.net

Across

2. unemotional; sluggish; dull

4. worst moment; the lowest point

5. a model or example/ a way of thinking

9. treacherous; not trustworthy

11. not well known/ unclear; difficult to understand

13. having small holes allowing substances to pass through; penetrable

15. an outcast

16. being charitable or generous

Down

1. bad tempered; rude or impatient; irritable

3. a beggar

5. transparent; clear

6. characterized by great variety or diversity

7. eager to give advice or services when they are not wanted; meddlesome

8. unimportant; not worth considering

9. keen at perceiving and understanding; sharp witted

10. rich or wealthy

11. noisy and difficult to deal with; defiant

12. transparent; clear

13. a loyal supporter/ devoted

14. gloomy or expressing sadness

Section 7 Multiple Choice Review

Fill in the blank with the best answer.

1. Ryan grew _____ and began to weep after learning that his dog had died while he was at work.
   a. morose   b. pallid   c. petulant   d. pellucid

2. Compared to her excitable twin sister, Rosa's _____ personality is surprising to most people.
   a. multifarious   b. negligible   c. noisome   d. phlegmatic

3. The long-running Republican _____ stopped campaigning for governorship after his criminal history was made public.
   a. mendicant   b. nadir   c. pariah   d. partisan

4. The music of The Rolling Stones appeals to a(n) _____ audience of all ages and races.
   a. philanthropic   b. phlegmatic   c. multifarious   d. negligible

5. Being defeated in the talent contest was the _____ of Chris's musical career.
   a. paradigm   b. pariah   c. nadir   d. partisan

6. The bank robber had to dispose of all his _____ connections because he did not want to get caught.
   a. philanthropic   b. permeable   c. perfidious   d. obscure

7. Because the difference between the two performances was _____, it was decided that both musicians should receive the top award.
   a. obstreperous   b. perfidious   c. perspicacious   d. negligible

8. The music concert was cancelled for _____ reasons which no one understood.
   a. obscure   b. noisome   c. multifarious   d. perspicacious

9. The other kids made John a(n) _____, refusing to play with him because he smelled bad.
   a. mendicant   b. paradigm   c. pariah   d. partisan

10. After losing their parents, the poor children had no option but to beg for food like _____ .
    a. pariahs   b. mendicants   c. paradigms   d. partisans

11. The student's _____ and argumentative nature made him a perfect candidate for the debate team.
    a. opulent   b. obstreperous   c. obscure   d. multifarious

12. The water _____ jacket provided little protection against the rain.
    a. pellucid   b. permeable   c. pallid   d. obscure

13. The family's _____ lifestyle was partially intended to make their neighbors jealous.
    a. officious   b. opulent   c. perspicacious   d. philanthropic

14. Kirsten was looking forward to going on vacation in order to tan her _____ skin.
    a. pellucid   b. permeable   c. pallid   d. phlegmatic

15. In the engineering class, students were encouraged to think beyond the old _____ to develop a new mechanism that runs on an alternative energy source.
    a. pariahs   b. partisans   c. nadirs   d. paradigms

16. The children could easily see several fish in the _____ lake because it was crystal clear.
    a. pellucid   b. officious   c. opulent   d. pallid

17. Sandy found she had a "green thumb" after proving to be a(n) _____ student in the horticulture class.
    a. multifarious   b. obstreperous   c. perspicacious   d. negligible

18. The _____ dog had to be put outside for the day because he was behaving so badly.
    a. officious   b. phlegmatic   c. pellucid   d. petulant

19. He donated two years of his time to the _____ organization to help less fortunate people.
    a. philanthropic   b. officious   c. noisome   d. petulant

20. The _____ police man asked the speeding driver all types of prodding questions into his personal life before giving him a ticket.
    a. perfidious   b. officious   c. phlegmatic   d. pallid

Section 7 Matching Review

Match the word on the left to the correct meaning on the right.

1. _____ Mendicant
2. _____ Morose
3. _____ Multifarious
4. _____ Nadir
5. _____ Negligible
6. _____ Obscure
7. _____ Obstreperous
8. _____ Officious
9. _____ Opulent
10. _____ Pallid
11. _____ Paradigm
12. _____ Pariah
13. _____ Partisan
14. _____ Pellucid
15. _____ Perfidious
16. _____ Permeable
17. _____ Perspicacious
18. _____ Petulant
19. _____ Philanthropic
20. _____ Phlegmatic

A. unimportant; not worth considering
B. a model or example/ a way of thinking
C. gloomy or expressing sadness
D. a loyal supporter/ devoted
E. worst moment; the lowest point
F. an outcast
G. treacherous; not trustworthy
H. eager to give advice or services when they are not wanted; meddlesome
I. a beggar
J. unemotional, sluggish, dull
K. noisy and difficult to deal with; defiant
L. characterized by great variety or diversity
M. having small holes allowing substances to pass through; penetrable
N. being charitable or generous
O. bad tempered; rude or impatient; irritable
P. rich or wealthy
Q. keen at perceiving and understanding; sharp witted
R. transparent; clear
S. lacking color or liveliness
T. not well known/ unclear; difficult to understand

Section Eight

'plA-"kAt or 'pla-"kAt

(Verb) to soothe; to prevent anger

Keyword: play cake

To **placate** her father after he returned home grumpy from a hard day's work, the little girl gave him a **play cake** of rocks and dirt.

The shop owner attempted to **placate** his angry workers with higher wages and better benefits.

Since the last court date, in late June, [the company] and its lawyers had been involved in negotiations to **placate** those who appear to oppose the reorganization plan.[281]

If Stockings to Stuf runs out of a product, Weiner relies on his staff to **placate** the customer and make the sale.[282]

write your own: |

Ponderous

'pän-d&-r&s   or 'pän-dr&s

(Adjective) heavy or weighty/ slow or awkward because
something is heavy or large/ boring or unpleasantly dull
Keyword: pond

His steps seemed **ponderous** as he struggled to move the
heavy and awkward **pond**.

The teacher's slow and **ponderous** delivery made the lecture
even more monotonous.

Ian Forrest succeeds in adapting Lewis Carroll's sometimes
ponderous prose into a magical theatrical evening at the
Theatre by the Lake.[283]

In a faster-moving world, this **ponderous** linear activity [of
management] breaks down. It is too slow. It is not well enough
informed with real-time information.[284]

write own:

Precocious

pri-'kO-sh&s

(Adjective) prematurely advanced, especially in children
Keyword: free coaches

The **precocious** young chess player was given **free coaches** when he began training for the world championship.

Justin's teachers decided the **precocious** child was so smart she could skip the next two grades.

A sickly, **precocious** child, [French physicist, mathematician and theologian Blaise Pascal] had been closeted from other children and educated by his scientist father, who discovered that the eleven-year-old Blaise had secretly worked out for himself the first twenty-three propositions [math proofs] of Euclid ["father" of Geometry].[285]

Precocious and prolific, Hargrove was 20 when he cut his first record as a leader, won the Down Beat Readers' Poll ... and captured a Grammy last year....[286]

write your own:

Pretentious

pri-'tent-sh&s or pri-'ten-sh&s

(Adjective) claiming or giving the appearance of unjustified importance or distinction
Keyword: pretend

George acted **pretentious** when he **pretended** to be a war hero, but in reality he was a coward.

Movie critics are often viewed as a **pretentious** group because their opinions are often presented as facts.

Orchids may seem to be the **pretentious**, stunning and oh-so-demanding supermodels of the flower world. But it's not so, say enthusiasts.[287]

They complain that the director of [the movie] Ocean's Eleven is being **pretentious** by working fast and cheap.[288]

write your own: |

pri-'var-&-"kAt

(Verb) to lie or to evade [dodge] the truth
Keyword: prepare a cake

Grandma **prepared a cake** after her granddaughter **prevaricated** and told her that she had finally graduated.

When the principal cornered the bully about fighting, he **prevaricated** and denied he was involved.

It's the people with no integrity who get all the opportunities to **prevaricate** for top dollar while an honest man..., who would genuinely feel a great deal of remorse, guilt and bowel agitation should he ever have to cut ethical corners to grab the big score, is not given the chance.[289]

He never for a moment tries to **prevaricate** or evade, even when the account casts him in an extremely dubious [questionable] light.[290]

write own:

Proclivity

prO-'kli-v&-tE

(Noun) a tendency or inclination towards
a particular thing
Keyword: no activity

Taylor had a **proclivity** for **no activity**, sleeping his life away.

Nancy's **proclivity** for drinking and pool playing is not acceptable to many of the people in her small town.

Working 16-hour days, six or seven days a week, he has put his concern for his patients above his personal life. Slightly rumpled, with a **proclivity** for bow ties, he yawns a lot.[291]

They are now faced with an extremely disillusioned [disappointed] investor base that shows no **proclivity** to become enlightened [informed] anytime soon.[292]

write your own:

Profusion

pr&-'fyü-zh&n or prO-'fyü-zh&n
(Noun) large amount/ extravagance
Keyword: more fuse on

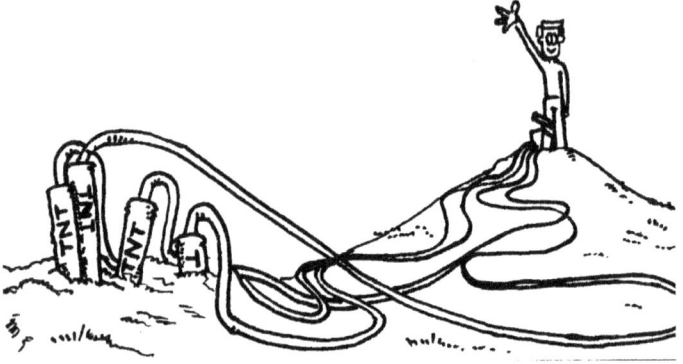

Afraid that the dynamite would explode too quickly, he put **more fuse on**, creating a **profusion** of fuse line.

The Girl Scouts sold such a **profusion** of Girl Scout cookies that it took them two weeks to deliver them.

Among a **profusion** of tips about how to choose from a restaurant menu and entertaining at home, her book supplies abundant advice on returning to the dieter's path, based on hard-won experience.[293]

At one time, the grass on the Boston Common [one of the oldest public parks in the USA] could hardly be seen for the **profusion** of woolly backs of sheep.[294]

write your own:

                    http://SolidA.net

Propitious

pr&-'pi-sh&s

(Adjective) favorable or advantageous/ gracious
Keyword: propeller

With the enormous high powered **propeller**, the sleek boat was in a **propitious** position to win the race.

Judging by the business received on the opening day of the small grocery store, it seemed that the location was a **propitious** choice.

She owes it all to **propitious** seating. "At an Los Angeles charity dinner for the homeless," she explains, "I sat next to a woman who was a producer for MTV." One thing led to another, and several months later Melissa wound up with her gig.[295]

After a series of **propitious** chemical explosions [Smith discovered] how to produce what is known as recombinant DNA.... Rewriting, in effect, the chemical code of life.[296]

write own:

Proselytize

'prä-s&-l&-"tIz or 'prä-sl&-"tIz

(Verb) to convert to a particular religion,
lifestyle or cause
Keyword: pretzel for fries

The doctor **proselytized** better eating habits, trying to convert restaurants to switch **pretzels for fries**.

The couple was arrested for **proselytizing** their religious beliefs in a country where it was illegal.

He keeps his eyes on a very different prize, opting instead to try to **proselytize** his peers.[297]

Zelnick had to **proselytize** to get his executives to use email—the entertainment business is not, he says, computer literate—but "there's nothing like the CEO to go on email for people to use it."[298]

write your own: |

                    http://SolidA.net

Protract

prO-'trakt or pr&-'trakt

(Verb) to prolong or extend
Keyword: protractor

The kids moaned with despair as they believed that using **protractors** in math would **protract** the class period into their recess.

Brian **protracted** the romantic date with his girlfriend by offering to take her out for ice cream after the concert.

Tuck your chin so your head is in line with your body, and pull your toes toward your shins. **Protract** your shoulder blades while keeping your belly button drawn in.[299]

As to your expectations of a favorable answer from the Onondagas [Native American tribe], we must desire you to cut off your hope, and not **protract** it to any farther length; for we know by experience that hope deferred is very painful.[300]

write your own: |

Pugnacious

"p&g-'nA-sh&s

(Adjective) quarrelsome; eager to fight
Keyword: bug faces

The **pugnacious** boy made so many **bug faces** at me that I was eager to fight him.

Alice's **pugnacious** speech against the nuclear power plant brought the crowd to an angry frenzy.

She has a **pugnacious** nature and becomes ever more angry as a fight progresses.[301]

In short, we should be willing to use boycott, threat, confrontation, censure, tirade, nearly anything, to retaliate. I don't consider myself **pugnacious** by nature, but I actively advocate such belligerent [hostile] actions because in a way I am at war with the exploiters....[302]

write your own:

  http://SolidA.net

Pundit

'p&n-d&t

(Noun) a person who is an authority on a subject;
of great learning/ a critic
Keyword: nun kit

The new nuns were excited after a religious **pundit** created
nun kits for their training.

Nick was known as the trading card **pundit** in my class. He
knew the exact value of all of his cards and all of the major
league players' statistics.

To sell their books, tapes, and seminars, these **pundits** promised the masses a solution to their dilemma.[303]

Pundits can talk and talk and talk, using this piece of data
and that bit of evidence to assure the American public that
this is all going to play out in our favor.[304]

write your own: |

Quandary

'kwän-d&-rE or 'kwän-drE

(Noun) a puzzling or perplexing situation

Keyword: laundry

The roommates were in a **quandary** after finishing the **laundry** because they had to determine whose socks were whose.

The increased violence in schools has left many parents in a **quandary** about where to educate their children.

This is the **quandary** the Kearneys still face. Should they let their gifted son just be Michael, or should they suppress his advanced abilities so that he will fit in socially?[305]

But captive breeding [of North American elephants] is fraught with physical obstacles and philosophical **quandaries**.[306]

write your own:

©Solid A, Inc.   http://SolidA.net

Raconteur

"ra-"kän-'t&r or "ra-"k&n-'t&r

(Noun) storyteller
Keyword: wreck on tour

The judge ordered the **raconteur** to take his **wreck on tour**. He had to drive his beat up car around the country, telling his story.

Around the campfire, the scoutmaster proved to be a brilliant **raconteur**, keeping the children spellbound with his stories.

One day in the waning years of his life, Red Pollard stopped talking. Perhaps it was a physical problem. Perhaps the old **raconteur** just didn't want to speak anymore.[307]

Rare as story talent is, we often meet people who seem to have it by nature, those street-corner **raconteurs** for whom storytelling is as easy as a smile.[308]

write your own: |

Ramify

'ra-m&-"fI

(Verb) to divide or branch out
Keyword: rams

The **rams** forged new trails in the mountains, **ramifying** the existing former path into several branches.

The tourists were bewildered when the freeway seemed to **ramify** into several different roads at once.

For the next fifty years the park would remain "the great focus of travel, from which speedy communications will **ramify** in all directions."[309]

Mushrooms differ from plants in several ways. The part we eat is only one small portion of the organism, most of which lives invisibly underground as a fine, cottony network of fibers, or hyphae, which **ramify** through the soil to gather nutrients.[310]

write your own: |

©Solid A, Inc.   http://SolidA.net

Rancor

'ra[ng]-k&r or 'ra[ng]-"kor

(Noun) a feeling of hostility and hatred
Keyword: rank her

The ice skating judges disagreed so much when they had to **rank her** in the competition that the **rancor** among them led to open hostility and fighting.

The parents continuously looked for ideas to stop the hostility and **rancor** among their children.

For years now, presidential appointments to federal courts have been mired [entangled] in partisan squabbling. But the **rancor** between Democrats and Republicans hit a new level this week.[311]

There is a growing disconnect and a widening chasm [gap] of disbelief, suspicion and **rancor**.[312]

write your own:

'rAz

(Verb) to destroy or to level
Keyword: raisin

The **raisins razed** the raisin factory, destroying it in order to stop their families from being boxed and eaten.

The earthquake **razed** and leveled much of the city, leaving it in disrepair.

The Duke of Brunswick, commander of the Prussian armies, issued a manifesto demanding that we release the king and restore all royal powers, or his troops would **raze** Paris to the ground.[313]

When word of the appointment [of a tax collector for the Stamp Act] reached America, it incited [stirred up] an angry mob, which marched on his house, ready to **raze** it.[314]

write **own:** your

Rebuff

ri-'b&f

(Verb) to refuse or to snub/
(Noun) sharp refusal
Keyword: re-buff

The car owner **rebuffed** the worker for missing some spots and refused to pay until the car was **re-buffed** again.

The principal refused to listen and **rebuffed** all recommendations to cut the music program.

Elizabeth Blackwell got her medical degree in 1849, having overcome many **rebuffs** before being admitted to Geneva College.[315]

If it had been a domestic situation, it would have been called stalking, but as this was Parliament, it was simply the Trade Minister refusing to stop pestering the United States for a free trade deal, despite a firm **rebuff**.[316]

write your own: |

Recluse

're-"klüs or ri-'klüs

(Noun) withdrawn or secluded person
Keyword: real close

The **recluse** would not allow anyone to get **real close** to him by living in a cabin far away from anyone.

Emily Dickinson, a great American poet who was considered a **recluse**, was rarely seen outside the confines of the family estate.

[He] could not cope with human beings and became a **recluse** who communicated only with his poodle, Atman.[317]

Maier describes how, over the years, [a man] transformed himself from a **recluse** into a powerful executive, an arbiter of taste and a potent force in the worlds of politics, journalism, fashion, literature, and art.[318]

write your own:

Relic

're-lik

(Noun) a thing or part that remains from the past
Keyword: relish

An amazing **relic**, the **relish** jar from the Last Supper, was discovered in the archaeological dig.

The kids poked fun of Bob's old car, calling it a **relic** from the 1960's.

Catherine had always had an interest in ancient Egyptian artifacts and reproductions of **relics** from that period.[319]

Beginning tomorrow, Drexel University in Philadelphia will draw upon the China National Silk Museum in Hangzhou for a show of 60 robes, cloth samples and other **relics** from the Han dynasty in the third century B.C. to the Qing dynasty in the 19th century.[320]

write your own: |

Section 8 Crossword Puzzle

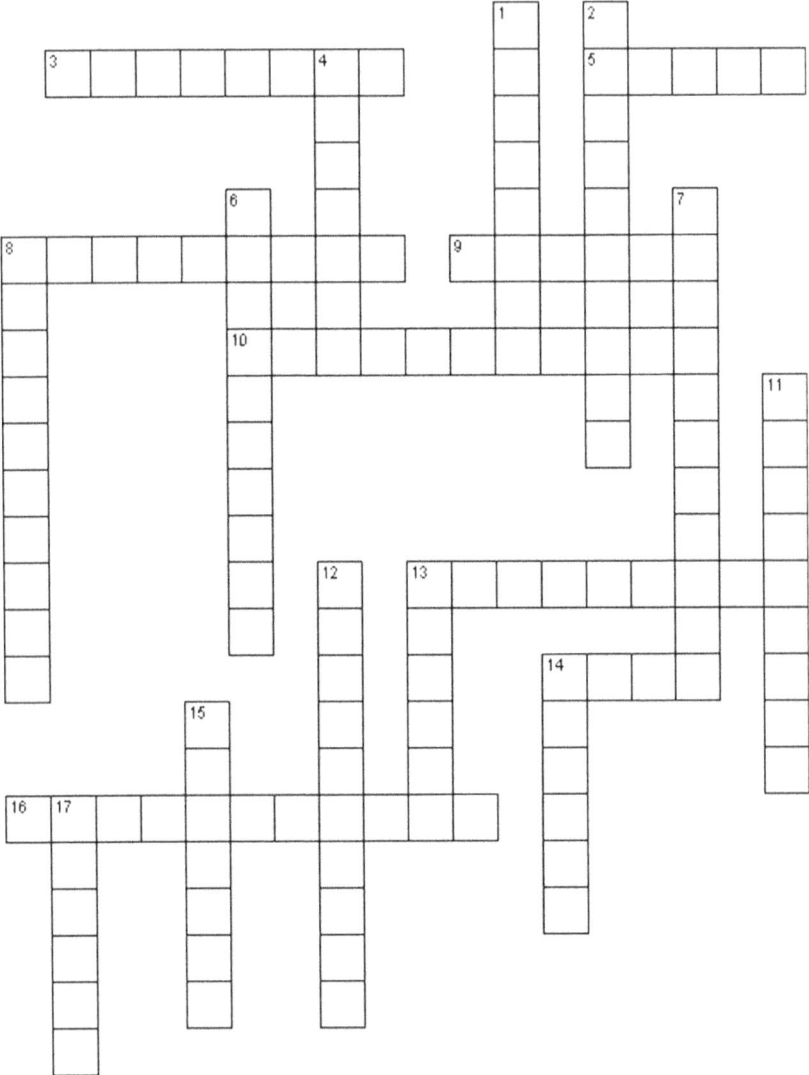

©Solid A, Inc.   http://SolidA.net

Across

3. a puzzling or perplexing situation

5. a thing or part that remains from the past

8. heavy or weighty/ slow or awkward/ boring or unpleasantly dull

9. a feeling of hostility and hatred

10. claiming or giving the appearance of unjustified importance or distinction

13. large amount/ extravagance

14. to destroy or to level

16. to lie or to evade [dodge] the truth

Down

1. to prolong or extend

2. prematurely advanced, especially in children

4. withdrawn or secluded person

6. favorable; advantageous/ gracious

7. to convert to a particular religion, lifestyle or cause

8. a tendency or inclination towards a particular thing

11. storyteller

12. quarrelsome; eager to fight

13. a person who is an authority on a subject; of great learning/ a critic

14. to divide or branch out

15. to soothe; to prevent anger

17. to refuse; to snub/ sharp refusal

Section 8 Multiple Choice Review

Fill in the blank with the best answer.

1. The _____ young lady felt she knew more about art then her professor.
    a. pretentious   b. propitious   c. ponderous   d. pugnacious

2. After 50 years in prison, the old man seemed like a _____, continuing to perform tasks the old fashioned way.
    a. pundit   b. raconteur   c. rancor   d. relic

3. As a result of his _____ for criminal behavior he was continuously sentenced to jail.
    a. quandary   b. rancor   c. proclivity   d. profusion

4. She _____ him even though he begged for forgiveness on bended knee.
    a. razed   b. rebuffed   c. proselytized   d. placated

5. Sharon knew it was not going to be a _____ day after being woken up four times in the middle of the night by her two year old.
    a. propitious   b. pugnacious   c. pretentious   d. ponderous

6. Although Gail did not like her friend's haircut, she could not tell her friend the truth and _____ when her friend asked if she liked her new style.
    a. placated   b. prevaricated   c. ramified   d. rebuffed

7. The life of the automobile was _____ by taking it in for regular oil changes and for scheduled service maintenance.
    a. prevaricated   b. placated   c. protracted   d. ramified

8. The teachers identified the boy as a bully because of his _____ attitude; he was always looking for a fight.
    a. precocious   b. protractive   c. reclusive   d. pugnacious

9. His book never reached the best-seller list due to his _____ writing style.
    a. precocious   b. pugnacious   c. ponderous   d. pretentious

10. It's hard to get an appointment with my hair stylist if you are not a regular customer, as she is considered a cosmetology _____.
    a. pundit   b. relic   c. raconteur   d. recluse

11. Unable to decide which movie to rent, Samantha spent over an hour in the video store in a _____.
a. profusion   b. quandary   c. rancor   d. relic

12. The film-maker attributed his success to his skill as a _____, with a natural ability for weaving a good tale.
a. recluse   b. raconteur   c. pundit   d. quandary

13. The meeting erupted in _____ when individuals with opposing ideas started yelling and pointing fingers.
a. profusion   b. proclivity   c. pundit   d. rancor

14. The newspaper article angered him so much; it took a long time to finally _____ him.
a. rebuff   b. placate   c. protract   d. raze

15. Though the people living in the commune were very happy with their lifestyle, they never tried to _____ other people into sharing their lifestyle if they weren't interested.
a. placate   b. proselytize   c. prevaricate   d. ramify

16. They _____ the old office building in order to build a new hotel at the same location.
a. razed   b. rebuffed   c. protracted   d. placated

17. The _____ of selections in the fifty page lunch menu was overwhelming, making it very difficult for most people to order.
a. quandary   b. proclivity   c. pundit   d. profusion

18. Hiding in what they thought was an old abandoned house, the children were sure the _____ was a ghost since none of them had seen him before.
a. pundit   b. raconteur   c. recluse   d. profusion

19. Although the _____ new college graduate seemed inexperienced, his skills and expertise were very advanced despite his young age.
a. propitious   b. ponderous   c. pretentious   d. precocious

20. His troubles _____ as his lie branched out into a series of problems.
a. proselytized   b. prevaricated   c. ramified   d. razed

Section 8 Matching Review

Match the word on the left to the correct meaning on the right.

1. _____ Placate
2. _____ Ponderous
3. _____ Precocious
4. _____ Pretentious
5. _____ Prevaricate
6. _____ Proclivity
7. _____ Profusion
8. _____ Propitious
9. _____ Proselytize
10. _____ Protract
11. _____ Pugnacious
12. _____ Pundit
13. _____ Quandary
14. _____ Raconteur
15. _____ Ramify
16. _____ Rancor
17. _____ Raze
18. _____ Rebuff
19. _____ Recluse
20. _____ Relic

A. prematurely advanced, especially in children
B. to convert to a particular religion, lifestyle or cause
C. quarrelsome; eager to fight
D. a person who is an authority on a subject; of great learning/ a critic
E. large amount/ extravagance
F. heavy or weighty/ slow or awkward/ boring or unpleasantly dull
G. a puzzling or perplexing situation
H. to prolong or extend
I. a thing or part that remains from the past
J. favorable; advantageous/ gracious
K. to soothe; to prevent anger
L. withdrawn or secluded person
M. to refuse; to snub/ sharp refusal
N. storyteller
O. a feeling of hostility and hatred
P. claiming or giving the appearance of unjustified importance or distinction
Q. to lie; to evade the truth
R. to divide or branch out
S. a tendency or inclination towards a particular thing
T. to destroy or to level

Section Nine

Repudiate

ri-'pyü-dE-"At

(Verb) to reject or to disown; to refuse to recognize
Keyword: pew date

She **repudiated** her **pew date** and refused to see him again after he swore in church when she asked him to pass the Bible.

The workers **repudiated** the new contract offer, and refused to go to work until their demands were recognized.

She had navel and nasal rings, dyed hair, and a chain-smoking habit, all to **repudiate** adult mores [rules]. She had also joined a rather bizarre group of dissident aging teens, virtually none of whom, I suspect, had earned a reputation for high academic output.[321]

To him, Harrison represented the old Chicago of filth, smoke, and vice [corruption], everything the fair was designed to **repudiate**.[322]

write your own:

©Solid A, Inc.   http://SolidA.net

Retrograde

're-tr&-"grAd

(Adjective) having a backward motion or direction
Keyword: grade

Instead of helping the student's **grades**, the tutor had a **retrograde** effect on the child's school work.

Though Tommy was an exceptional student, his mother did not want him to skip ahead a grade, fearing that it would create a **retrograde** effect on his social life.

But the trauma to her brain caused **retrograde** amnesia, erasing virtually her entire memory of the previous 18 months—including any recollection of the man she had fallen in love with and married.[323]

[Meriwether] Lewis hated to turn around. "This is the first time since we have been on this long tour that we have ever been compelled to retreat or make a **retrograde** march.--Lewis and Clark Expedition"[324]

write your own:

Ribald

'ri-b&ld, 'ri-bold, or ''rI-''bold

(Adjective) characterized by crude or indecent joking; vulgar
Keyword: real bald

The kids loved to tell **ribald** jokes about the man's **really bald** head.

William had a tendency to tell **ribald** jokes at church, and was consequently avoided.

In New Jersey, for example, when a drunken Republican editor was charged with making a **ribald** reference to the president's posterior [buttocks], the jury returned a not guilty verdict on the grounds that truth was a legitimate defense.[325]

Blonde, with intense, staring eyes, she could be disorienting silent in company and then, after a few drinks, **ribald**, witty, and by all accounts irresistible.[326]

write your own:

©Solid A, Inc.   http://SolidA.net

Sagacity

s&-'ga-s&-tE or si-'ga-s&-tE

(Noun) good judgment; wisdom
Keyword: Sack City

Due to the **sagacity** of its leaders, sacks were recycled over and over again in **Sack City**.

Wendy was voted president of the student council due to her **sagacity** and good judgment on tough issues.

Showing measured restraint, skill with young talent and strong storytelling sense … [he] brings **sagacity** and sympathy to "Antwone Fisher," a fictionalized drama....[327]

While man has sometimes succeeded in dragging the dog down to his level, the dog has only occasionally succeeded in raising man to his level of **sagacity**. –James Thurber[328]

write your own:

Salutary

'sal-y&-"ter-E

(Adjective) beneficial; improving
Keyword: salute

It is very **salutary** to **salute** the colonel in order to show respect for command and to avoid punishment.

Flunking the pretest was a **salutary** reminder that he needed to study more.

Wachtler's compassion for the other prisoners and his newly reconsidered ideas about the injustices of our legal system almost make one think it might be **salutary** for other judges to do a little hard time....[329]

Among other things, [Florence] Nightingale taught the British army about the **salutary** effects of sunlight, pure water, and clean kitchens. In two and a half years, the mortality rate among troops in England was cut in half.[330]

write your own: |

     http://SolidA.net

Sanguine

'sa[ng]-gw&n

(Adjective) cheerful, confident or optimistic
Keyword: penguin

The **sanguine penguin** was the biggest attraction at the zoo because he seemed so cheerful and upbeat.

Trying not to get his hopes up, Oscar was still secretly **sanguine**, feeling he had an excellent chance of getting the job promotion.

Arnold's former police chief … was **sanguine** this week as he discussed his chances of being reinstated [put back on the police force].[331]

[Former Olympic medalist Jenny] Thompson wasn't as **sanguine** as she seemed. Watching the [Olympic] individual events go off was agony.[332]

write own:

'sa-ch&-"rAt

(Verb) to soak thoroughly; to fill fully or to capacity
Keyword: sat and ate

Larry **sat and ate** in the rain until his clothes were totally **saturated** with water.

The stadium was **saturated** with people as the rock concert was completely sold out.

He's been flooding stores with his product, and he's proud of the fact. "We were afraid we'd **saturate** the market, but everything's been selling so hot, it's amazing," he says.[333]

There is a maxim [fundamental principle] in the advertising business that an advertisement has to be seen at least six times before anyone will remember it. That's a useful lesson for Coca-Cola or Nike, who can afford to **saturate** all forms of media....[334]

write your own:

Scoff

'skäf or 'skof

(Verb) to express scorn or mockery
Keyword: cough

The doctor **scoffed** at the boy's fake **cough**.

Years ago people would have **scoffed** at the idea that nearly every home would have a small personal computer.

When I tell people I do 20 minutes of aerobic exercise, they **scoff**, "Is that all?"[335]

No actual documentation of its authenticity exists other than local hearsay [gossip], and some historians **scoff** at the idea that the 1809 cabin has survived. But the thousands of annual visitors to the Abraham Lincoln Birthplace and National Historic Site seem satisfied that they are viewing a typical home of the area in the Lincoln era, if not the authentic building.[336]

write your own:

Scrutinize

'skrü-t&n-"Iz

(Verb) to examine carefully
Keyword: screw-in eyes

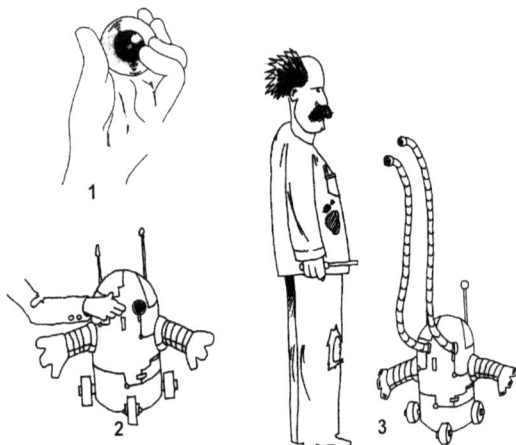

The robot did not like what he saw when he **scrutinized** the professor's sloppy appearance with his **screw-in eyes**.

The doctor **scrutinized** the cut and discovered an infection.

He had a file and I guess my photograph was in it. He looked in the file and **scrutinized** my face for a moment.[337]

It may be the quality and quantity of an applicants' high school coursework that receives the closest **scrutiny** at the more prestigious institutions, but these are cumulative [added together] indicators of performance.[338]

write your own: |

Sectarian

sek-'ter-E-&n

(Adjective) narrow-minded/ strongly supporting or related to a particular religion or sect

Keyword: secretary

The **secretaries** took their jobs too seriously and created a **sectarian** group that strongly supported and revered the head secretary, Jan.

Wars sparked by **sectarian** differences are an enigma, as religion should promote peaceful resolutions.

The religious and political passions which ravaged the British Empire during the whole reign of Charles I drove fresh crowds of **sectarians** every year to the shores of America.[339]

Ramona would have had to realize that something about her speech, whether its manner or its content, had upset the prejudices, superstitions, or narrow **sectarian** beliefs of the note's writer.[340]

write your own:

Sequester

si-'kwes-t&r

(Verb) to remove or set apart/
to put into isolation
Keyword: pester

Because Cecilia was **pestering** her little brother, her mother **sequestered** her to her bedroom for the afternoon.

At the airport, the customs officials **sequestered** illegal animal products entering the country.

In the 19th century, the rich began to **sequester** themselves in neighborhoods from Gramercy Park in New York to the Central West End in St. Louis.[341]

Attorneys for [the] sniper suspect ... are asking a Fairfax County judge to appoint five criminal investigators to help them prepare for his capital murder trial and may seek to **sequester** the jury....[342]

write your own:

Serendipity

"ser-&n-'di-p&-tE

(Noun) a pleasant, accidental discovery
Keyword: Seven dips

It was a case of **serendipity** when the chef accidentally tripped and spilled his **seven dips** together which resulted in his world famous chip dip.

In 1928, Alexander Fleming made the **serendipitous** discovery of penicillin when he noticed that a culture plate containing bacteria was contaminated by mold.

In a classic example of **serendipity**, a survey originally designed to improve the way astronomers estimate the distance to elliptical galaxies has now revealed large-scale bulk motions among the galaxies.[343]

Whether or not it was **serendipity**, the initial sighting of Chang [later to become a world class tennis player] came at an indoor tennis club ... The pint-size youngster was running through drills with his older brother....[344]

write own: |

Sophistry

'sä-f&-strE

(Noun) clever use of reasoning or argumentation
that seems true but is false
Keyword: sofa history

ELVIS PRESLEY SOLD THIS COUCH TO MARTIN LUTHER KING!

The sellers used clever **sophistry** to sell the sofa, making up an elaborate story about the **sofa's history**.

Until the true facts were uncovered, his **sophistry** fooled many people.

The **sophistry** of this argument fairly filled me with rage. I knew not how to counter such nonsense.[345]

When he was forty years of age, and after he had been a member of Congress, he studied Euclid so that he [Abraham Lincoln] could detect **sophistry** and demonstrate his conclusions. [346]

write your own:

Sporadic

sp&-'ra-dik

(Adjective) occurring at irregular intervals of time; scattered

Keyword: sports-addict

Because he was a **sports-addict**, his attendance at school was **sporadic**. He rarely came to class when his favorite teams were playing.

The village relied on a **sporadic** electrical supply that was available only a few hours a day.

During long but **sporadic** creative periods, Zelda Fitzgerald painted grotesque ballerinas with large feet....[347]

A deeply ironic play, Romulus elicited only **sporadic**, isolated chuckles from a baffled audience, and had me fleeing at the interval.[348]

write your own: |

Stultifying

(Verb*) to limit or render useless and ineffectual/ to make something appear stupid or foolish

*Stultifying is a verb that functions like an adjective

Keyword: stilts flying

The "**Stilts Flying**" stunt was a **stultifying** feat, effectively ending his career as a stunt man.

She felt that playing the musical scales repetitively had a **stultifying** effect on her musical creativity, because she was not getting any better.

She had been brought up in the strict, **stultifying** tradition of the Nieto family ... If you were a woman, that you devoted your entire existence to your husband and children.[349]

A thirty-five-year old mother of three, married to a controlling, **stultifying**, inflexible, chauvinistic husband, gradually and painfully comes to realize that her dependency on him and their marriage is a living death.[350]

write own:
your

---

240   ©Solid A, Inc.   http://SolidA.net

Stymie

'stI-mE

(Verb) to hinder or obstruct; to check or block
Keyword: sty (pig pen)

The child's bedroom was such a pig **sty** that the clutter **stymied** his mother's attempt to enter the room to tuck him in at night.

Her older brother got in her way and **stymied** her attempt to get the last slice of cheesecake.

Inevitably such [company policy] manuals are collections of "don'ts." And "don'ts" stop initiative [ambition], squelch innovation [origin creations], **stymie** creativity.[351]

During week 2 ... you will also learn how to avoid some of the common pitfalls that can **stymie** your progress.[352]

write your own: |

Substantiate

s&b-'stant-shE-"At

(Verb) to prove, to confirm or to support
Keyword: sub stand she ate

Under cross examination, the detective **substantiated** that he found her fingerprints at the **sub stand** where **she ate**.

The fact that cigarettes cause cancer has been **substantiated** by numerous studies.

He says Foster had thrown a soda bottle at Henson's car on the interstate and had spit on Henson at the exit. (So far, investigators have been unable to **substantiate** those claims.)[353]

All this helped to reline and further **substantiate** her initial theory, making her case ... even more convincing.[354]

write your own: |

©Solid A, Inc. http://SolidA.net

Sullen

's&-l&n

(Adjective) gloomy/ silently resentful
Keyword: swollen

His **swollen** eye made him feel **sullen** and resentful towards his friend for hitting him.

Our waitress' gloomy mannerism matched her **sullen** expression.

It made me contemplate how anyone could be so malicious [spiteful] to another person, and for a few hours after we left, I felt very bitter. The whole experience was **sullen**.[355]

The child becomes **sullen**, refuses to interact, and may sit in a corner, hugging a doll or sucking a thumb.[356]

write own:

Superficial

(Adjective) shallow/ concerned with only
the obvious or surface
Keyword: super official

He only looked like a **super official**, but in reality his knowledge of the game was **superficial**.

Compared to the tragedies aired on the world news, many of the stories on the local news are relatively **superficial**.

Whether it was with colleagues and direct reports at the office or with his wife and child at home, he felt that his connections were disturbingly thin and **superficial**.[357]

Such issues, she insists, are only "the **superficial** reasons" for her belief. She says the real basis for her faith is "spiritual."[358]

write own:

©Solid A, Inc.   http://SolidA.net

Supersede

"sü-p&r-'sEd

(Verb) to take the place of; to replace
Keyword: super seed
Note: also spelled "supercede"

Jack's **super seed** outgrew and **superseded** all of the beanstalks in the garden and reached up through the clouds.

Setting a new record in the men's 400 meter race, Jose **superceded** Samuel as the school's All Star Athlete.

My authority comes from the attorney general and **supercedes** that of your chief of police.[359]

At what point does an athlete's personal business become our business? When does a fan's right to know **supercede** the right to privacy?[360]

write your own: |

Section 9 Crossword Puzzle

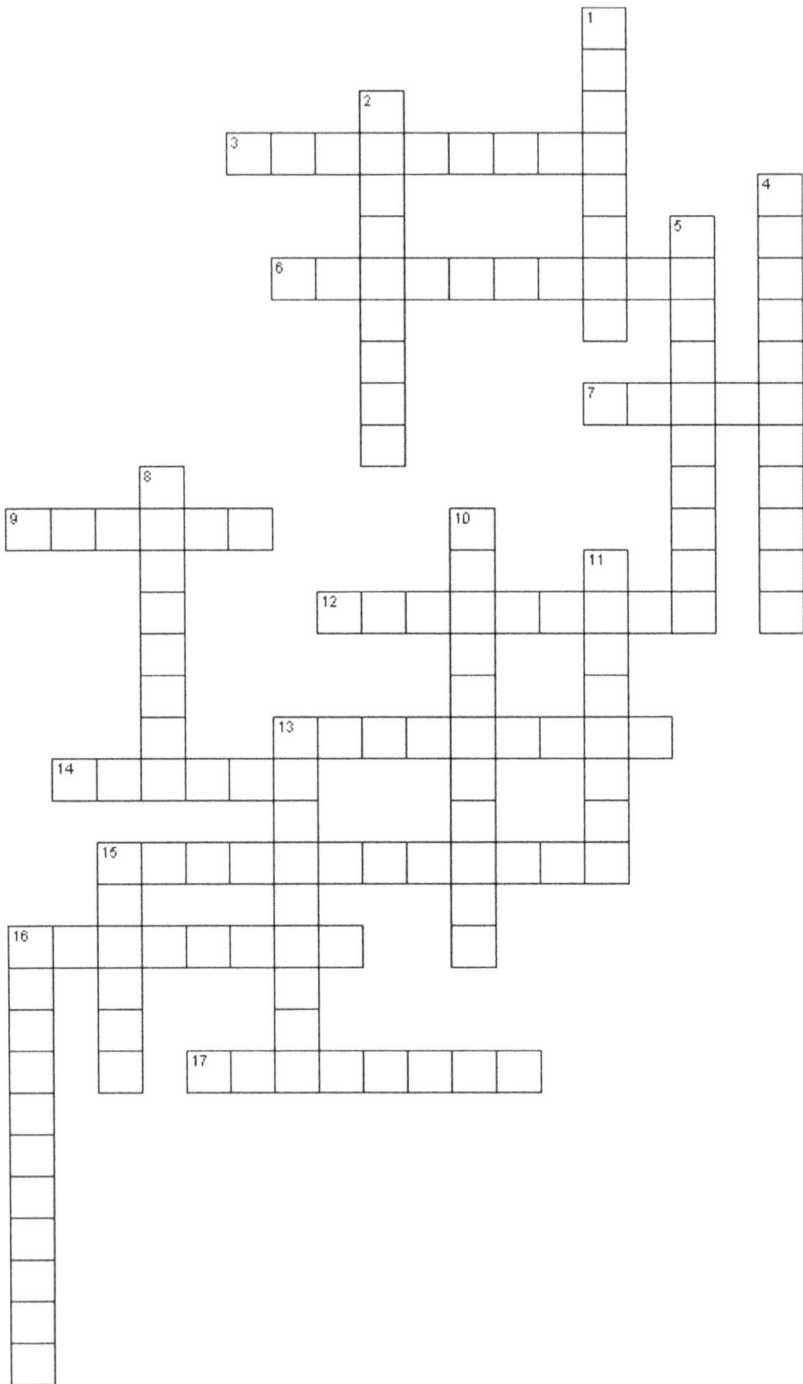

©Solid A, Inc.   http://SolidA.net

Across

3. to remove or set apart/ to put into isolation

6. to examine carefully

7. to express scorn or mockery

9. characterized by crude or indecent joking; vulgar

12. to reject or to disown; to refuse to recognize

13. clever use of reasoning or argumentation that seems true but is false

14. to hinder or obstruct; to check or block

15. to prove; to confirm; to support

16. beneficial; improving

17. cheerful, confident or optimistic

Down

1. occurring at irregular intervals of time; scattered

2. to take the place of; to replace

4. shallow; concerned with only the obvious or surface

5. having a backward motion or direction

8. good judgment; wisdom

10. to limit or render useless and ineffectual; to make something appear stupid or foolish

11. to soak thoroughly; to fill fully or to capacity

13. narrow-minded; strongly supporting or related to a particular religion or sect

15. gloomy; silently resentful

16. a pleasant, accidental discovery

Section 9 Multiple Choice Review

Fill in the blank with the best answer.

1. The _____ politician always considered what he was going to say before speaking in order to portray his ideas correctly.
   a. sanguine   b. superficial   c. ribald   d. sagacious

2. Accusations against the pop singer have not been _____ or credibly supported.
   a. superficial   b. repudiated   c. substantiated   d. sequestered

3. Though computers allow for more free and constant communication, some may argue that it is less personal, and therefore a _____ step in human interaction.
   a. retrograde   b. salutary   c. substantiated   d. sanguine

4. The constant rain completely _____ the ground with water.
   a. repudiated   b. stymied   c. superseded   d. saturated

5. When the prisoner acted up, he was _____ to the isolation cell for 48 hours.
   a. sequestered   b. stymied   c. retrograded   d. superseded

6. The applicant's _____ character made him unfit, in the eyes of the school, to work with children.
   a. sanguine   b. salutary   c. ribald   d. sullen

7. Vicky was _____ about finally being released from the hospital and began to plan what she wanted to do when she arrived home.
   a. sullen   b. sanguine   c. sagacious   d. ribald

8. Although the accident looked horrific, the passengers were lucky as they only sustained _____ injuries.
   a. sullen   b. retrograde   c. sporadic   d. superficial

9. The _____ experience of the near drowning in the pool left all the life guards more cautious and alert.
   a. salutary   b. sporadic   c. serendipitous   d. sagacious

10. The new sign being built is to _____ the old, rusty one formerly used by the company.
    a. saturate   b. supersede   c. substantiate   d. sequester

11. Computer networks were _____ after computer viruses overloaded servers with too much email.
    a. stymied   b. scrutinized   c. scoffed   d. superseded

12. Although many people _____ at the initial idea, the invention eventually made a fortune.
    a. scoffed   b. sequestered   c. stultified   d. superseded

13. Many believe that _____ education is essential for promoting specific values and morals.
    a. stultifying   b. superficial   c. sectarian   d. substantiated

14. Lisa often told people that finding her husband was a true case of _____; they literally bumped into each other.
    a. serendipity   b. sagacity   c. repudiation   d. sophistry

15. The lawyer's _____ won him the case, but he later felt guilty about the erroneous statements he made to gain victory.
    a. substantiation   b. sophistry   c. saturation   d. stultification

16. The math club had a few _____ meetings throughout the school year.
    a. sequestered   b. sectarian   c. sporadic   d. serendipitous

17. His _____ comment made everyone feel stupid.
    a. sectarian   b. salutary   c. serendipitous   d. stultifying

18. Because the Ugly Duckling looked different, his siblings _____ him and refused to swim near him.
    a. scrutinized   b. repudiated   c. saturated   d. stultified

19. The sky looked _____ with dark gray clouds.
    a. sanguine   b. stymied   c. saturated   d. sullen

20. After _____ the test, Jane felt as though she should have studied more.
    a. repudiating   b. scrutinizing   c. scoffing   d. sequestering

Section 9 Matching Review

Match the word on the left to the correct meaning on the right.

1. _____ Repudiate
2. _____ Retrograde
3. _____ Ribald
4. _____ Sagacity
5. _____ Salutary
6. _____ Sanguine
7. _____ Saturate
8. _____ Scoff
9. _____ Scrutinize
10. _____ Sectarian
11. _____ Sequester
12. _____ Serendipity
13. _____ Sophistry
14. _____ Sporadic
15. _____ Stultifying
16. _____ Stymie
17. _____ Substantiate
18. _____ Sullen
19. _____ Superficial
20. _____ Supersede

A. to express scorn or mockery
B. to take the place of; to replace
C. good judgment; wisdom
D. to prove, to confirm, or to support
E. to examine carefully
F. clever use of reasoning or argumentation that seems true but is false
G. gloomy; silently resentful
H. having a backward motion or direction
I. narrow-minded; strongly supporting or related to a particular religion or sect
J. characterized by crude or indecent joking; vulgar
K. occurring at irregular intervals of time; scattered
L. to hinder or obstruct; to check or block
M. cheerful, confident or optimistic
N. a pleasant, accidental discovery
O. shallow; concerned with only the obvious or surface
P. to reject; to disown; to refuse to recognize
Q. beneficial; improving
R. to limit or render useless and ineffectual; to make something appear stupid or foolish
S. to soak thoroughly; to fill fully or to capacity
T. to remove or set apart/ to put into isolation

Section Ten

Surmise

s&r-'mIz or 's&r-" mIz

(Verb) to guess based on little evidence
Keyword: sunrise

Ancient legends **surmised** the origin of the **sunrise** by creating elaborate stories that were based on little evidence.

With no one living who speaks the language, archaeologists are only able to **surmise** the meaning of the ancient hemitropic writings.

Why is excess salt bad for some of us? Researchers **surmise** that the problem originated in the early days when humans lived in a low-salt, high potassium environment.[361]

Many scholars have **surmised** that the Medes launched a surprise attack on the city when the fierce Assyrian military was fighting elsewhere.[362]

write your own: |

Surreptitious

"s&r-&p-'ti-sh&s or s&-"rep-'ti-sh&s

(Adjective) done in secret; hidden
Keyword: syrup dishes

When no one was looking, John **surreptitiously** allowed his dog to help wash the **syrup dishes** by licking them clean.

The teacher knew that Jimmy could hardly wait for recess when he noticed his **surreptitious** glance at the clock.

Her payload deposited, the lady scurries away to meet co-conspirator June—she doesn't want her full name revealed—at a white Volkswagen parked a block distant. Now it's June's turn to do the **surreptitious** feeding [of the pigeons]. [363]

In films, magazines, books, music and fashion imagery, the cigarette has become a standard fixture, emerging not from the **surreptitious** promotional efforts of tobacco multinationals but from a perception that "smoking is cool again."[364]

write your own:

Sycophant

'si-k&-f&nt or 'si-k&-"fant

(Noun) one who flatters without sincerity

Keyword: sick of ants

The roach was **sick of ants** living like **sycophants** in his motel—always flattering him but rarely paying.

The family accused the young bride of being a **sycophant**—full of flattery but really only interested in the millionaire's money.

When the family business is rock stardom, however, the perks —international adoration, untold wealth, glamorous **sycophants**—might make taking after dear old dad a tad more palatable [acceptable].[365]

The special interests and the **sycophants** will stand in the rain a week to see you and will treat you like a king. They'll come sliding in and tell you you're the greatest man alive....[366]

write your own: |

Talon

'ta-l&n

(Noun) sharp claw, usually on a bird of prey
Keyword: tail on

Only a few reptiles had their **tails on** due to the fast **talons** on the bird of prey.

The hawk snatched the squirrel with his long, sharp **talons**.

Securing its hind legs in her relentless grip, [the eagle] attacks the fox's head, paralyzing her prey with **talon** tips exerting thousands of pounds of pressure per square inch.[367]

The fantasy elements of the property will include … the nest and **talon** of a giant Roc bird taken from the "Sinbad the Sailor" stories that will provide a dramatic backdrop to an overlooking bar.[368]

write your own: |

‘ten-y&-w&s

(Adjective) flimsy or weak/ can easily be proven false
Keyword: tennis

The **tenuous** relationship between the doubles partners in **tennis** was a sight to behold. One minute they were buddies, the next minute enemies.

The police made a **tenuous** connection between the two local robberies; however they did not have enough evidence to make an arrest.

Iraqi archaeologists have found **tenuous** evidence that the northern gate of the city was destroyed at about that time.[369]

And always there's the feeling that his once brilliant career—his life, really—has become nothing more than a spectacular display of dissolution [disintegration], a late-20th-century parable that warns us all how **tenuous** our talents are, how fragile our contract with civilization.[370]

write your own:

Thwart

'thwort

(Verb) to prevent or hinder
Keyword: wart

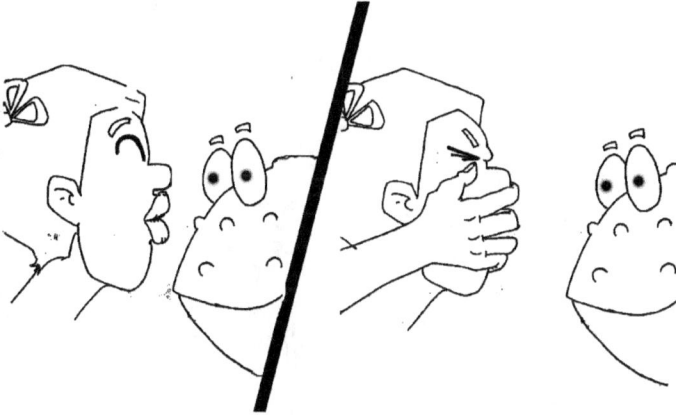

The mother **thwarted** her daughter's attempts to kiss the toad to prevent her from getting **warts**.

The police **thwarted** the robbers' plan to rob the bank by arresting them.

Most championship caliber softball teams send out one pitcher game after game and count on her to **thwart** the opposition.[371]

Designed to **thwart** counterfeiting, the new currency looks counterfeit itself.[372]

write own: |

Tirade

'tI-"rAd or 'ti-"rAd

(Noun) a long speech characterized
by anger and irritation
Keyword: tie raid

After the **tie raid**, the police chief launched into a long **tirade**, lecturing the crooks about selling counterfeit ties.

The mother launched into an angry **tirade** that lasted an hour after her son tracked mud into the house.

Lou Piniella is not a man known for his patience. In his new job as manager of the Tampa Bay Devil Rays, Piniella had better learn to develop some or we'll be seeing more of his famous on-field **tirades** than ever before.[373]

So far, most of Mercer's spleen-venting has occurred in his two-minute **tirades** in each installment of 22 Minutes [TV show], which began its sixth season this week.[374]

write your own: |

Transient

'tran-zE-&nt or 'tran-sh&nt

(Adjective) temporary or brief
Keyword: trance

Being hypnotized and put in a brief **transient trance** is a small price to pay for the possibility of a life long cure from tobacco addiction.

The **transient** storm blew through town, causing a great deal of damage in a short amount of time.

The city is building a marina for **transient** visiting boaters....[375]

Recorded in London with British musicians, it's a mature, assured song cycle that deals with the classic themes of the **transient** nature of love and existence.[376]

write your own: |

Truncate

'tr&[ng]-"kAt or 'tr&n-"kAt

(Verb) to shorten
Keyword: trunk

The stewardess **truncated** the man's **trunk** with a saw so it would fit into the overheard compartment on the plane.

Americans often like to **truncate** the first names of people. Pamela is referred to as Pam. Patrick becomes Pat.

While many merchants already **truncate** the 16-digit card numbers on receipts, Visa will require, beginning July 1, that new credit-card machines display only the last four digits....[377]

The [computer] program can **truncate** the password at 8 characters, so those extra 192 characters never get written into memory anywhere.[378]

write your own: |

Turpitude

't&r-p&-"tüd or 't&r-p&-"tyüd

(Noun) wickedness; shamefulness; a corrupt act
Keyword: turnip dude

The **turnip dude** spent five months in jail for his acts of **turpitude** which included throwing rotten turnips through windows.

George could almost always be found engaging in some activity of moral **turpitude**, from copying assignments or tests to cheating at any competitive game on the playground.

Moral **turpitude** on Herbert's part was inconceivable [unthinkable]. Whatever he was up to, it had to be for a good cause.[379]

Cobb County public school officials will discuss a system-wide conduct code today that would suspend any athlete from the team who is charged with a felony or "misdemeanor involving moral **turpitude**."[380]

write own:

Untenable

"&n-'te-n&-b&l

(Adjective) incapable of being maintained or defended
Keyword: ten cables

Even with the **ten cables**, the castle was **untenable** as the dragons easily invaded the fortress.

The theory that the earth was the center of the universe was **untenable** after Galileo's scientific observations of the heavens.

But the changing relationship between politicians and lawyers means that it is now simply **untenable** for one man both to make laws and to rule on them as a judge.[381]

[She] is placed in an **untenable** position ... She is the key witness to the death of a friend and must return his infant son to a family that is unaware of his existence.[382]

write your own: |

Utopian

yu-'tO-pE-&n

(Adjective) perfect or ideal/ impractical/
idealistic situations or scenario
Keyword: U toe piano

In a **utopian** society, everyone would be able to play incredible music on "**U**" shaped **Toe Pianos**.

With a **utopian** vision, Mohandas Gandhi was able to reduce the tensions and conflicts in India.

When envisioned by Walt Disney as a **utopian** working city of the future, EPCOT was the acronym for Experimental Prototype Community Of Tomorrow.[383]

It is safe to say that TC Boyle is not a great believer in **utopian** experiments. In previous novels, he has skewered improbable [unlikely] schemes such as cereal king John Harvey Kellogg's revolutionary health spa and a pioneering turn-of-the-century mental asylum [mental institution].[384]

write your own: |

'va-p&d or 'vA-p&d

(Adjective) dull, uninteresting or lacking liveliness
Keyword: rapids

The usually exciting **rapids** in the river were calm, making what once was our vacation highlight, a **vapid** experience.

The audience became bored with the dull and **vapid** performance of the actors in the theater production.

You think he's **vapid**, dim-witted, with his stupidity arising....[385]

Lara Merriken was on a hike, gnawing on a **vapid** energy bar, when inspiration struck. "Why isn't somebody making something that is healthy, tastes good, and is made with wholly unprocessed foods?" she asked herself.[386]

write your own:

Verbose

"v&r-'bOs or v&r-'bOs

(Adjective) wordy
Keyword: verbs

Chris is so **verbose**. He never runs out of **verbs** and is constantly talking.

The president of the chess club rebuked the members for talking too much and being **verbose**.

Harry never regained his ability to speak, but he was **verbose** in Morse code....[387]

Drivers would have had to pull over to read the sign, it was so **verbose**. On a highway, two words—maybe something catchy, like "Free Checking"—must be made to suffice.[388]

write your own: |

'vi-l&-"fI

(Verb) to speak evil of; to damage one's reputation by saying or writing something

Keyword: village fry

The **village fry** was **vilified** after everyone got sick.

The spy was **vilified** by the press for being a traitor.

MP3.com [attempted to argue in court] that Universal views it as a competitor and thus would like to "put it out of business or publicly **vilify** it...."[389]

In another story, "The Great Tiger with a Long Tail," a troop of monkeys gather to **vilify** the tiger of the title until they convince themselves that they have talked him to death.[390]

write your own:

Voluble

'väl-y&-b&l

(Adjective) talking with ease
Keyword: volleyball

The **voluble volleyball** players ended up talking for hours instead of playing their game.

Nobody would have guessed that English was not the first language of the **voluble** guest. He was so fluent, and talked with such ease.

Acid freaks [drug addicts who take acid] are not given to **voluble** hospitality; they stare fixedly at strangers, or look right through them.[391]

Given half the chance, Brian Gaines, a **voluble** sort never short on ideas, will tell you he has many identities: new father, husband, Noe Valley neighbor, nonprofit executive director, friend.[392]

write your own:

Voracious

vo-'rA-sh&s or v&-'rA-sh&s

(Adjective) extremely hungry, greedy or eager
Keyword: four races

After winning **four races**, he had a **voracious** appetite that was not easily satisfied.

Trevor is a **voracious** reader. It is a rare moment to find him without a book.

Voracious eaters, the larvae will consume anything they can swallow, including their hatching brothers and sisters.[393]

Picasso was such a **voracious** artist, and such a terrible show-off, that he made art even when relaxing at his favorite Paris restaurant, Le Catalan. All he needed was a paper tablecloth and some wine, mustard or coffee.[394]

write own:

Wither

'wi-[th]&r

(Verb) to shrivel/ to lose freshness/ to make speechless
Keyword: with her

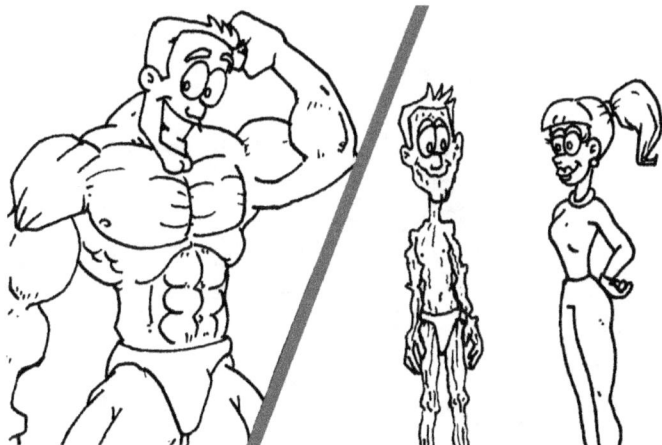

Whenever the body building champ is **with her**, he **withers**—shriveling up into a small speechless wimp.

The crops **withered** and died in the intense heat for lack of rain.

So many churches start off with life and vitality only to end in a split, or simply **wither** away and die.[395]

Some argue that, because of such emphasis on high-volumes, entertainment companies are more prone now to focus intently on middle-of-the-road material, leaving less marketable but more creative fare to **wither** on the vine.[396]

write your own: |

Writhe

(Verb) to twist or squirm (especially in pain)
Keyword: ride

The injured football player **writhed** and squirmed in pain during the bumpy **ride** on the stretcher.

Hercules **writhed** in pain after dropping the boulder on his foot.

His films are greenhouses, where the air is hung with a brew of unsettling aromas. Only rarely do fearful things jump out at you, preferring to grow and **writhe** at their own pace.[397]

American gardeners, who **writhe** like earthworms on hot asphalt in agonizing inferiority at the mere mention of English garden, tend to assume the British did it all and did it first.[398]

write your own:

Zealot

'ze-l&t

(Noun) a fanatic; a person who shows great
enthusiasm for a cause
Keyword: sell it

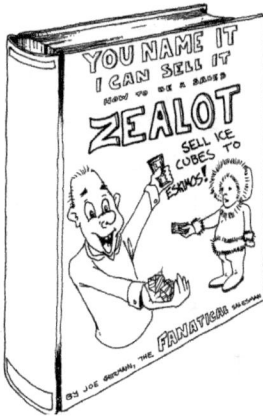

Learn to be a sales **zealot** by reading the enthusiastic book,
"You Name It, I Can **Sell It**."

Joan, a running **zealot**, refuses to take a day off, rain or shine.

Boston can be a rough place to play.... Slow starts are not
forgiven. You have to perform or the local sports **zealots**
jump all over you.[399]

She was a religious **zealot** who insisted he attend church services daily, and frequently accused him of sinful transgres-
sions.[400]

write your own: |

Section 10 Crossword Puzzle

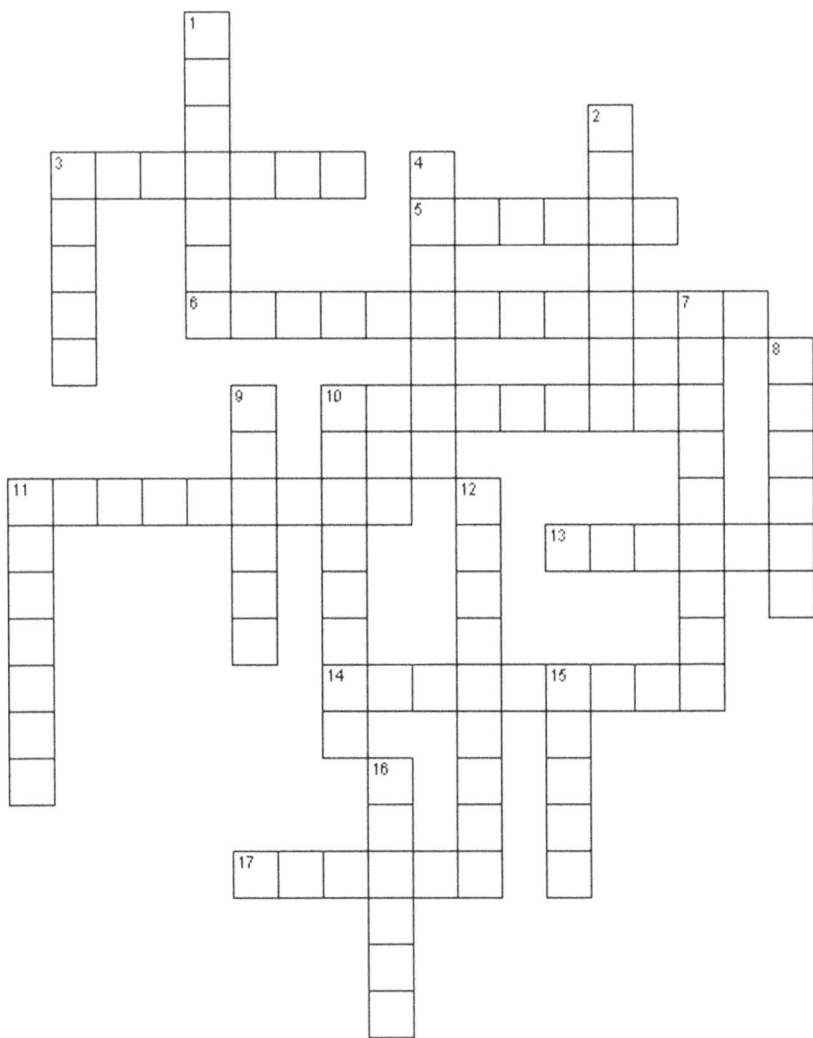

©Solid A, Inc. http://SolidA.net

Across

3. talking with ease

5. to prevent or hinder

6. done in secret; hidden

10. temporary or brief

11. extremely hungry; greedy or eager

13. a long speech characterized by anger and irritation

14. wickedness, shamefulness, or a corrupt act

17. a fanatic; a person who shows great enthusiasm for a cause

Down

1. flimsy or weak; can easily be proven false

2. to guess based on little evidence

3. dull or uninteresting; lacking liveliness

4. perfect or ideal/ impractical/ idealistic situations or scenario

7. incapable of being maintained or defended

8. to shrivel; to lose freshness/ to make speechless

9. to twist or squirm (especially in pain)

10. to shorten

11. wordy

12. one who flatters without sincerity

15. sharp claw, usually on a bird of prey

16. to speak evil of; to damage one's reputation by saying or writing something

Section 10 Multiple Choice Review

Fill in the blank with the best answer.

1. A doctor's shots help _____ illness.
   a. wither   b. tirade   c. thwart   d. vilify

2. Though the student worked very hard on the painting, it looked _____ and bland.
   a. vapid   b. voracious   c. untenable   d. voluble

3. Even though there was a rule about eating in the classroom, the teacher sneaked a _____ bite of a cookie when her students were not looking.
   a. transient   b. surreptitious   c. voracious   d. tenuous

4. Logging in the rainforests has been so _____ that only a small fraction of the original forests are left.
   a. voracious   b. vapid   c. thwarted   d. untenable

5. Sally's fake nails looked like _____ attacking the keyboard as she typed.
   a. sycophants   b. zealots   c. turpitudes   d. talons

6. With little evidence, the teacher _____ that the student must have cheated to get an "A" on the test.
   a. surmised   b. vilified   c. truncated   d. writhed

7. Although the school bully made a _____ agreement not to call names or fight on the school grounds, the students remained careful not to upset him.
   a. surreptitious   b. tenuous   c. verbose   d. vapid

8. I always questioned Jerry's motives when he complimented me because I had been warned that he was a _____.
   a. zealot   b. utopia   c. sycophant   d. talon

9. Her thoughts of running away to Europe for a year were _____; there were so many other things she also wanted to do.
   a. voluble   b. verbose   c. surreptitious   d. transient

10. The _____ sermon seemed to last forever.
    a. voluble   b. verbose   c. tenuous   d. truncated

11. The new calculator she purchased rounds or _____ numbers
    at the third decimal place.
    a. truncates   b. surmises   c. writhes   d. thwarts

12. The old sailor's face looked _____ and worn.
    a. writhed   b. withered   c. transient   d. vilified

13. The _____ of his opponents made the game unfair, since his
    team followed all the rules.
    a. tirade   b. turpitude   c. utopia   d. voracity

14. Students were _____ in their efforts to raise money to pre-
    serve the rainforest.
    a. tenuous   b. surreptitious   c. transient   d. zealous

15. The board's decision to fire the secretary was _____ after dis-
    covering someone else had stolen the money from the school of-
    fice.
    a. verbose   b. truncated   c. untenable   d. withered

16. The basketball player was benched for the duration of the game
    after he launched into an angry _____ with the referee for
    calling a foul on him.
    a. zealot   b. tirade   c. sycophant   d. talon

17. The emperor was happy to see the gladiator _____ in pain.
    a. withering   b. surmising   c. writhing   d. truncating

18. Many people pray for the _____ goal of world peace.
    a. voluble   b. vapid   c. surreptitious   d. utopian

19. The student was _____ by his classmates for his picking his
    nose.
    a. thwarted   b. withered   c. vilified   d. truncated

20. The television station looked for a _____ person to fill the
    new position of the talk show host.
    a. transient   b. untenable   c. utopian   d. voluble

Section 10 Matching Review

Match the word on the left to the correct meaning on the right.

1. _____ Surmise
2. _____ Surreptitious
3. _____ Sycophant
4. _____ Talon
5. _____ Tenuous
6. _____ Thwart
7. _____ Tirade
8. _____ Transient
9. _____ Truncate
10. _____ Turpitude
11. _____ Untenable
12. _____ Utopian
13. _____ Vapid
14. _____ Verbose
15. _____ Vilify
16. _____ Voluble
17. _____ Voracious
18. _____ Wither
19. _____ Writhe
20. _____ Zealot

A. a long speech characterized by anger and irritation

B. flimsy or weak; can easily be proven false

C. to prevent or hinder

D. temporary or brief

E. to guess based on little evidence

F. to shorten

G. talking with ease

H. a fanatic; a person who shows great enthusiasm for a cause

I. wickedness; shamefulness; a corrupt act

J. incapable of being maintained or defended

K. perfect or ideal/ impractical/ idealistic situations or scenario

L. dull or uninteresting; lacking liveliness

M. wordy

N. to speak evil of; to damage one's reputation by saying or writing something

O. to twist or squirm (especially in pain)

P. done in secret; hidden

Q. extremely hungry; greedy or eager

R. to shrivel; to lose freshness/ to make speechless

S. one who flatters without sincerity

T. sharp claw, usually on a bird of prey

Free Resources

Free Resources @ www.solida.net

Audio Recordings

Eliminate the worry of mispronouncing the words by listening to the online audio recordings .

Cartoon Animations

Watch select words from this book come to life in funny and memorable cartoon animations which are sure to make you smile.

Templates

Print or download the "Create Your Own" template to create your own VOCABBUSTERS for your own words.

Learning Style Assessment

Find out more about your learning or cognitive style by taking a free online assessment.

Vocabulary Resources

Discover other great free vocabulary and educational resources and links for teachers, parents and students which can also be accessed at this site.

Need more VOCABBUSTERS words?

VOCABBUSTERS Vol. 2 is now available!

Create Your Own

Word: _____

Defintion: _____

_____

Caption: _____

_____

Example Sentence: _____

_____

_____

_____

For a free downlad of this template, go to http://www.solida.net.

Example
Sentence
References

Example Sentence References

A. Parker, K. (4 December 2003). Cartoon harrumphers should loosen up. *The Witchita Eagle*, p. 11A[A]

B. Martel, Y. (2001). *Life of Pi*. Orlando, FL: Harcourt Books, Inc., p. 258.[B]

1. Stephan, A. (2003, March 6). It is now emerging that the Columbia space shuttle had serious problems on 20 of its 28 flights, and that a near-disaster in 1999 was hushed up. *New Statesman, 132*, 8.[1]

2. Adande, J.A. (2003, April 23). Lakers' Minnesota flats: No time to panic, but maybe that's the big problem. *Los Angeles Times*, Sports, p. 1.[2]

3. Urquhart, S. (2001, October 28). Scene fit for a drama. *Sunday Times*, Features.[3]

4. Stipp, D. (2003, February 3). The quest for the antifat pill. Nature programmed us to overeat. Fen-Phen helped that, until it backfired. Safer drugs may be coming soon. *Fortune, 147*, 66.[4]

5. Gang, C. A. (2002, December 4). Go ahead, have a dessert - A little treat here and there not such a big deal. *The Commercial Appeal* (Memphis, TN), p. E1.[5]

6. Limerick, P. N. (1999, June 20). Cheers! *New York Times*, p. 26.[6]

7. Ward, M. (1998, June 15). The infinitely tiny neutrino may give physics big reality check *Milwaukee Journal Sentinel*. Retrieved December 22, 2003, from JSOnline, http://www.jsonline.com/archive/news/0615matters.stm[7]

8. Collins, Jr., L. (2001, November 25). Simplifying, relativityly speaking. *The Houston Chronicle*, p. 19.[8]

9. Hunt, M. (2001, November 11). Being taken to school: Bucks are taught a painful lesson. *Milwaukee Journal Sentinel*, p. 01C.[9]

10. Stephen, A. (2002, December 16). Profile: Colin Powell. *New Statesman, 131*, 38.[10]

11. McLean, A. & Eldred, G. W. (2003*). Investing in Real Estate*. Hoboken, N.J.: John Wiley and Sons, Inc., p. 253.[11]

12. Monroe, V. (June 2003). How to raise the men we'd want to marry. *O Magazine*, p. 163.[12]

13. Williams, K. (2002, November 28). Love of Doo Wop gave birth to a business. *The Washington Post*, p. T05.[13]

14. Cochrane, D. (2003, July). Master of many media: John Wilson reveals and interprets the inner selves of the people he portrays using brush, graphite, clay, and etching tools. *American Artist, 67*, 56.[14]

15. Gay, N. (2003, January 1). Gannon's the best. *The San Francisco Chronicle*, p. C1.[15]

16. Snowman, D. (2003, January). Linda Colley: Daniel Snowman meets the historian of Britons and captives. *History Today, 53*, 18.[16]

17. Hudson, A. (1994). *The Historical Atlas of New York City: A Visual Celebration of Nearly 400 Years of New York City's History*. Markham, Ontario: Swanston Publishing Limited, p. 37.[17]

18. D'Epiro, P. (1998). *What Are the Seven Wonders of the World? and 100 Other Great Cultural Lists—Fully Explicated*. New York: Anchor Books, p. 185.[18]

19. Newfield, J. (2003, March 17). How the other half still lives; in the shadow of wealth, New York's poor increase. *The Nation, 276*, 11.[19]

20. Meek, J. (2002, August 20). Magic of mushrooms gets medical nod. *The Guardian*, p.5.[20]

21. Bryson, B. (2003). *A Short History of Nearly Everything*. New York: Broadway Books, p. 228.[21]

22. Jackson, D. D. (1985, April). Pursued in the wild for the pet trade, parrots are perched on a risky limb. *Smithsonian, 16*, 58-68.[22]

23. Cooper, I. (2003, January 1). Cohn, Rachel: The steps. *Booklist*, p. 887.[23]

24. Everson, D. (2003, April 21). Devs prepare to strike lightning. *Daily News* (New York), p. 67.[24]

25. Salinero, M. (2003, April 15). Marina gas tax favored to boost water police. *Tampa Tribune*, Metro, p. 1.[25]

26. Meers, E. & Rizzo, M. (1999, June 21). Bold act: Driven off TV by a stalker eight years ago, soap star Andrea Evans returns to work. *People Weekly, 51,* 121.[26]

27. Robson, J. (2003, May 22). They're changing hats at Buckingham Palace. A new exhibition explores the queen's taste in accessories. Julia Robson looks back on 50 years of remarkable headwear. *The Daily Telegraph,* p. 24.[27]

28. Butterfield, A. (2001, June 11). Prince of the city. *The New Republic,* p. 42.[28]

29. Phillips, D. T. (1992). *Lincoln on Leadership: Executive Strategies for Tough Times.* New York: Warner Books, Inc., p. 138.[29]

30. Bing, S. (1997, February 3). Stepping up to the firing line. *Fortune, 135,* 51.[30]

31. Fauber, J. (2003, December 5). Alcohol may not be food for brain. Study shows moderate use linked to atrophy. *Milwaukee Journal Sentinel.* Retrieved December 22, 2003, from JSOnline database.[31]

32. Weisman, J. & Keen, J. (2002, June 10). Bush plan would shift many with no role in security. *USA Today,* p. 5.[32]

33. Rowley, H. (2001, November 19). London after Bloomsbury. *The Nation, 273,* 28.[33]

34. Budick, A. (2003, April 20). Hidden treasures of the Met. *Newsday,* p. 20.[34]

35. Losos, J. (2003, March 2). The Righteous: The Unsung Heroes of the Holocaust. *St. Louis Post-Dispatch.* Retrieved December 22, 2003, from the St. Louis Post-Dispatch database.[35]

36. Stein, T. (2003, April 6). Second wave of lynx to be released in Colo. *The Denver Post,* p. B-03.[36]

37. Felton, V. (2003, June). 5 best towns: This year's top places to live and ride. *Bike Magazine, 10,* 38-44.[37]

38. Mannix, K. (2003, January 24). Football: Super bowl xxxvii: Buccaneers notebook: Gruden: It's all right in the family. *The Boston Herald,* p. 134.[38]

39. American Academy of Pediatrics (1991). *Caring for Your Baby and Young Child: Birth to Age 5.* New York, NY: Bantam Books, p. 348.[39]

40. Melton, R. H. (2003, February 3). Businessman and politics aren't mixing in Richmond. *The Washington Post,* p. 01.[40]

41. Gourevitch, A. (2003, March). Better living through chemistry: DDT could save millions of Africans from dying of malaria—if only environmentalists would let it. *Washington Monthly, 35,* 19-24.[41]

42. Abrashoff, Micheal (2002). *It's Your Ship: Management Techniques from the Best Damn Ship in the Navy.* New York: Warner Books, Back Cover.[42]

43. Morton, A. (1998). *Diana: Her True Story in her Own Words.* New York: Simon and Schuster, Inc., p. Front Matter.[43]

44. England, T. (2003, June 8). E-Books rise slowed, but they're here. *The Santa Fe New Mexican.* Retrieved December 22, from the Santa Fe New Mexico database.[44]

45. Pollard, S. (2002, September 18). Saddam is more than welcome to George Galloway. *The Times* (London), p. 20.[45]

46. Moore, L.W. (1997, October 4). No contest: Corporate lawyers and the perversion of justice in America. *America, 177,* 33.[46]

47. Jarvis, J. (1985, February 25). A bunny's tale. *People Weekly, 23,* 9.[47]

48. Black, J. (2003, February). Georges I and II limited monarchs: Jeremy Black reminds us of the importance of two of Britain's less well-loved monarchs. *History Today, 53,* 11-8.[48]

49. Patterson, K. (2002). *Crucial Conversations: Tools for Talking When Stakes are High.* New York: McGraw Hill, p. 66.[49]

50. Pay up, young'uns: German universities. (2003, May 10). *The Economist,* 367.[50]

51. Milligan, S. (2002, July 25). The nation: House votes to expel Traficant: Ohio democrat is second ousted since Civil War. *The Boston Globe,* p. 2.[51]

52. Castle, T. (2002, October 14). Art with a proper stranger. *The New Republic, 227,* 28.[52]

53. Another pipe bomb found in woods area. (1999, June 22). *The Boston Globe,* p.8.[53]

54. She's here to fix the xerox. (2001, August 6). *Business Week, 3744,* 47.[54]

55. Morre LaRoe, L. (1996, April). The Aran Islands: Ancient hearts, modern minds. *National Geographic, 189,* 118-34.[55]

56. Mistakes come back to haunt pataki: The state legislature delivered the governor a political black eye last week. Many say it was the governor's own doing. (2003, May 19). *Buffalo News,* p. A-1.[56]

57. Anderson, D. (2003, May 12). Movies. Sydney Morning Herald, *The Guide,* p.14.[57]

58. Hendrick, B. (2003, April 4). War in the Gulf. Overview: Battle for Baghdad: "Forget the Rambo stuff." *The Atlanta Journal*-Constitution, p. 12A.[58]

59. Upfront. (2003, March 8). *Billboard,* p. 9.[59]

60. Buckingham, M. (1999). *First, Break All the Rules: What the World's Greatest Managers Do Differently.* New York: Simon and Schuster, p. 59.[60]

61. Carnegie, D. (1984*). Stop Worrying and Start Living.* New York: Simon and Schuster Inc, p. 99.[61]

62. Rogers, M. (2003, May 11). Pawlenty plucks a pike promptly. Success came in first hour in fishing opener. *Star Tribune,* p. 6B.[62]

63. Watson, T. (1997, April 21). Snake! In search of the wild anaconda. *U. S. News and World Report, 122,* 80.[63]

64. Dell'Apa, F. (2003, May 11). Revolution 2, Galaxy 0 soccer: Revolution pick up win, consolation. *The Boston Globe,* p. 10.[64]

65. Thompson, M. (2000). *Raising Cain: Protecting the Emotional Life of Boys.* New York: The Ballantine Publishing Group, p. 99.[65]

66. Krakauer, J. (2003). *Under the Banner of Heaven: A Story of Violent Faith.* USA: DoubleDay, p. 27.[66]

67. Whitman, C. (2002, August 26). A strong climate plan. *Time, 160,* A48.[67]

68. Granatstein, L. (2003, May 19). Spring cleaning: Real simple eyes fashion fixes. *Mediaweek, 13,* 48.[68]

69. Dolgun, A. (1975) *Alexander Dolgun's Story.* New York: Alfred A. Knopf, Inc., p. 41.[69]

70. Abel, D. (2003, May 16). Veterans' shelter audit details mismanagement of funds. *The Boston Globe,* p. 5.[70]

71. Herbert, B. (2003). *The Machine Crusade* (Dune Series). New York: Tom Doherty Associates, LLC, p. 609.[71]

72. Walsh, K. (2001, January 8). Bush Inc. gets going. *U. S. News and World Report, 130,* 10.[72]

73. Nesselson, L. (2003, April 21). Echelon: The secret power. *Variety, 390,* 27.[73]

74. Brown, D. (1998). *Digital Fortress.* New York: St. Martin's Press, p. 106.[74]

75. Johnson, D. (2002, August 16). Boston radio: Hub stations struggle with ads, 9/11 programming. *The Boston Herald,* p. 31.[75]

76. Phillips, D. (1996, July). Coming of age. *Entrepreneur, 24,* 98.[76]

77. Wolf Shenk, J. (1996, March). The public schools' last hurrah? *Washington Monthly, 28,* 8.[77]

78. Maxwell, J. C. (1999). *The 21 Indispensable Qualities of a Leader: Becoming the Person Others Will Want to Follow.* Nashville, TN: Thomas Nelson, Inc., p. 2.[78]

79. Martin, L. (1991, April). Mr. Bowman's solution. *Saturday Evening Post, 263,* 46-53.[79]

80. Ingraham, Laura. (2007). *Power to the People.* Washington, DC: Regnery Publishing, p. 92.[80]

81. Daily News Yale (2003). *The Insider's Guide to the Colleges 20(30th Ed.).* New York: The Yale Daily News Publishing Company, Inc./St. Martin's Press, p. 208.[81]

82. McChesney, R. W. & Nichols, J. (2003, February 24). Media democracy's moment: Suddenly, there are widespread discussions about the dangers of monopoly power. *The Nation, 276,* 16.[82]

83. Lepage, M. (2003, May 30). Minis are the stars in high-class caper. Donald Sutherland does his thing as veteran safecracker, then rats out his gang. Look out. *The Gazette*, p. D1.[83]

84. Marshall Goldsmith, Marshall and Reiter, Mark (2007). *What Got You Here Won't Get You There: How Successful People Become Even More Successful.* New York: Hyperion, p. 47.[84]

85. Balzar, J. (2003, April 25). The land of the bilked, home of the corrupt. *Newsday*, p 41.[85]

86. O'Reilly, B. (2003). *Who's Looking Out for You?* New York: Random House, Inc., p. 119.[86]

87. Card, O. S. (1991). *Ender's Game.* New York: Tom Doherty Associates, LLC, p. 139.[87]

88. Vosepka, R. (2003, May 22). "Shocking" Fish Tale Surfaces on Utah's Green River. *The Santa Fe New Mexican.* Retrieved December 22, 2003, from The Santa Fe New Mexican database.[88]

89. Delavier, Frederic (2006). *Strength Training Anatomy*. Human Kinetics: Champaign, I, Back Cover.[89]

90. Funderburg, L. (2003, January 5). A sparkling life. *Newsday*, p.28.[90]

91. Portman, J. (2003, January 21). The Fuehrer furore: Many people have attacked the movie Max, but Noah Taylor—who plays the young Hitler—tells Jamie Portman it's a valuable lesson in how evil takes root in a human being. *Ottawa Citizen*, p. B7.[91]

92. Gilman, S. J. (2001). Kiss *My Tiara: How to Rule the World As a Smartmouth Goddess.* New York: Warner Books, Inc., p.171.[92]

93. Schouten, H. (2003, April 10). Mill town. *The Dominion Post*, Features, General p. 5.[93]

94. Whiteside, K. (2002, August 20). Vol has "unfinished business." *USA Today*, p. 3C.[94]

95. Andrews, P. (1994, October). The press. *American Heritage*, *45*, 36.[95]

96. Hamilton, J. (1986, December 15). A California doctor delivers good news to new moms with postpartum blues: It's curable. *People Weekly*, *26*, 101.[96]

97. Wilson-Smith, A. (2000, May 29). Gentleman Jean Beliveau. *Maclean's*, p.12[97]

98. Williams, J. (2003, April 25). Ed Burns tries to regain his confidence: His first step to regain some box-office clout: Star in other people's movies. *St. Louis Post-Dispatch* (Missouri), p. E1.[98]

99. Horn, R. (2002, April 1). Putting a permanent lid on Pol Pot. *Time International*, *159*, 4.[99]

100. Biederman, C. (1997, October 7). Subheadline: Temper temper. *Dallas Observer*. retrieved December 17, 2003, from http://www.dallasobserver.com/issues/1997-10-02/feature.html/1/index.htm[100]

101. Wilson, J. (2000, November). How I became a Jew, sometimes. *Books and Culture*, *6*, 5.[101]

102. Marshall Goldsmith and Reiter, Mark (2007). *What Got You Here Won't Get You There: How Successful People Become Even More Successful.* New York: Hyperion, p. 81.[102]

103. Rice, A. (1985). *Beauty's Release: The Sequel to the Claiming of Sleeping Beauty and Beauty's Punishment.* New York: Penguin Group, p. 145.[103]

104. Melton, R. H. (2003, January 9). Easygoing new speaker unlikely to find the going easy. *The Washington Post*, p. T04.[104]

105. Mills, M. (1996, September 26). Body and soul. *People*, *2*, 36.[105]

106. Breathnach, S. B. (1995). *Simple Abundance: A Daybook of Comfort and Joy.* New York: Warner Books, Inc., p. 31.[106]

107. The Hill: Senate GOP split over rules change on filibusters. (2003, May 14). *US Newswire*.[107]

108. Pryor, K. (1999). *Don't Shoot the Dog! The New Art of Teaching and Training.* New York: Bantam Books, p. 70.[108]

109. Acredolo, L. (2000). *Baby Minds: Brain-Building Games Your Baby Will Love.* New York: Bantam Books, p. xix.[109]

110. Martel, Y. (2001). *Life of Pi*. Orlando, FL: Harcourt Books, Inc., p. 14.[110]

111. Habib, D. (2002, May 6). Inside the NHL. *Sports Illustrated, 96*, 78.[111]

112. Goleman, D. (1995). *Emotional Intelligence: Why It Can Matter More Than IQ*. New York: Bantam Books, p. 131.[112]

113. Chase Lapine, Missy (2007). *The Sneaky Chef: Simple Strategies for Hiding Healthy Foods in Kids Favorite Meals*. Running Press: Philadelphia, PA, p. 203.[113]

114. Covey, S. R. (1989). *Seven Habits of Highly Effective People*. New York: Fireside, p. 93.[114]

115. MTV's World. (2002, February 18). *Business Week*, p. 40.[115]

116. Pedulla, T. (2003, May 13). Jockey lands on feet again. *USA Today*, p. 1.[116]

117. Rothwell, N. (2003, May 24). Anything but black and white. *The Weekend Australian*, p. 25.[117]

118. Martel, Y. (2001). *Life of Pi*. Orlando, FL: Harcourt Books, Inc., p. 275.[118]

119. Berry, L. L. (1999). *Discovering the Soul of Service: The Nine Drivers of Sustainable Business Success*. New York: The Free Press, p. 40.[119]

120. Greene, Robert (2000). *The 48 Laws of Power*. New York: Viking Penguin, p. 328.[120]

121. Mortenson, Greg and Oliver Relin, David (2007). *Three Cups of Tea: One Man's Mission to Promote Peace . . . One School at a Time*. New York: The Penguin Group, p. 157.[121]

122. Baker, K. (2001, November-December). Our town: We've seen it (almost) all before. *American Heritage, 52*, 20.[122]

123. Gabaldon, D. (1991). *Outlander*. New York: Dell Publishing, p. 140.[123]

124. Lane, A. (2003, March 31). The prime minister. *The New Yorker, 79*, 034.[124]

125. Kucherawy, D. (1991, August 12). Mao II. *Maclean's, 104*, 43.[125]

126. Bryson, B. (2003). *A Short History of Nearly Everything*. New York: Broadway Books, p. 103.[126]

127. Melton, E. (2002, October 1). Ashford, Jeffrey. A truthful injustice. *Booklist, 99*, 302.[127]

128. Ellis, Joseph. (2002). Founding Brothers: The Revolutionary Generation. Vintage Books: New York: Vintage Books, p. 135.[128]

129. Pollack, W. (1999). *Real Boys: Rescuing Our Sons from the Myths of Boyhood*. New York: Henry Hold and Company, LLC, p. 243.[129]

130. Bolton, R. (1979). *People Skills*. New York: Simon and Schuster, Inc., p. 51.[130]

131. Yerxa, D. (2002, May). The small chill: Rediscovering climate's impact on history. *Books and Culture, 8*, 40.[131]

132. Schulman, H. (2002, July 7). Giants rise up big time. *The San Francisco Chronicle*, p. B1.[132]

133. Editors of World Almanac (2004). *The World Almanac and Book of Facts 2004*. New York: World Almanac Education Group, Inc., p. 90.[133]

134. Goleman, D. (1997). *Emotional Intelligence: Why It Can Matter More Than IQ*. New York: Bantam Books, p. 80.[134]

135. Newman, C. (1997, June). Cats: Nature's masterwork. *National Geographic, 191*, 54.[135]

136. Henry, G. (2001, February). Knowledge, learning, and experience. *American Artist, 65*, 24.[136]

137. Gokavi, M. (2001, November 28). Alter coach, two players receive all-state honors; Domsitz co-coach of the year' Mangold, Getty make first team. *Dayton Daily News*.[137]

138. Neill, M. (1993, December 13). An angel looks homeward. *People Weekly, 40*, 79-81.[138]

139. Ban Breathnach, S. (1995). *Simple Abundance: A Daybook of Comfort and Joy*. New York: Warner Books, Inc., p. 102.[139]

140. Robertson, D. (2003, May 26). Given time to ponder, Ausmus sees positives. *The Houston Chronicle*, Sports, p. 9.[140]

141. Reed, J. D., Swertlow F., Clark C., Sheff-Cahan, V., & Francis, E. (2002, April 15).

142. Kidder, David S. and Oppenheim, Noah D. (2006). *The Intellectual Devotional: Revive Your Mind, Complete Your Education, and Roam Confidently with the Cultured Class*. New York: Rodale, Inc. , p. 162.[142]

143. Verducci, T. (2001, December 17). The power of two: Spurring each other on Curt Schilling and Randy Johnson carried Arizona to victory in the World Series and enthralled a nation. *Sports Illustrated*, *95*, 112.[143]

144. Klawans, S. (1995, June 26). Cannes '95. *The Nation*, *260*, 936.[144]

145. Hildebrand, J. (2003, May 1). Schooled in patience. *Newsday*, p. A03.[145]

146. Celia, F. (2002, November-December). De-stress to decrease risk of diabetes: Exercise and diet aren't enough. *Psychology Today*, *35*, 30.[146]

147. Doyle, A. C. (2002). *The Complete Sherlock Holmes*. New York: Random House, p. 427.[147]

148. McCullough, D. (2001). *John Adams*. New York: Simon and Schuster, p. 256.[148]

149. Frum, D. (June 16, 2003). What's right. *National Review*, *55*, 56.[149]

150. Carnegie, D. (1984). *How to Stop Worrying and Start Living*. New York: Pocket Books, p. 100.[150]

151. Shapiro, L. M. (2002, August 15) Expunge him. Letters from the issue of Thursday, August 15, 2002. *Dallas Observer*. Retrieved December 17, 2003 from http://www.dallasobserver.com/issues/2002-08-15/letters.html/1/index.html.[151]

152. Bolch, B. (2003, February 16). Shrine Games: Pete Rose's career is a featured attraction in Cooperstown, even though he remains ineligible for the Hall of Fame. *Los Angeles Times*, p. 1.[152]

153. Krakauer, Jon (1999). *Into Thin Air: A Personal Account of the Mt. Everest Disaster*. New York: Anchor Books, p. 233.[153]

154. Beattie, Melody (1992). *Codependent No More: How to Stop Controlling Others and Start Caring for Yourself*. USA: Hazelden Foundation, p. 64.[154]

155. Dolgun, A. (1975) *Alexander Dolgun's Story*. New York: Alfred A. Knopf, Inc., p. 200.[155]

156. Darrach, B. (1987, December 14). Grand old Lillian Gish makes a big splash in The Whales of August. *People Weekly*, *28*, 70-5.[156]

157. O'Reilly, B. (2003). *Who's Looking Out for You?* New York: Broadway Books, p. 150.[157]

158. Quackenbush, T. R. (1999). *Relearning to See: Improve Your Eyesight - Naturally!* Berkeley, CA: Frog, Ltd, p. 328.[158]

159. Auletta, K. (2002, June 10). The Howell Doctrine. *The New Yorker*.[159]

160. Aetna: A long way to the recovery room. (2001, July 16). *Business Week*, p. 56.[160]

161. Adcock, J. (2002, October 14). '21 Shots' abounds in oddity but lacks coherence. *Seattle Post Intelligence*. (Seattlepi.com). Retrieved December 17, 2003, from http://seattlepi.nwsource.com/theater/90856_shotsq.shtml?searchpagefrom=1&searchdiff=431.[161]

162. Kidder, Tracy (2004). *Mountains Beyond Mountains: The Quest of Dr. Paul Farmer, a Man Who Would Cure the World*. New York: Random House:, p. 96.[162]

163. Performing Arts. (2003, May 21). *The Washington Post*, p. C11.[163]

164. Scheib, R. (2003, January 13). Almodou. *Variety*, *389*, 46.[164]

165. Weber, D. (2003, February 20). Lopez lawyer files briefs blasting call for ouster as judge. *The Boston Herald*, p. O18.[165]

166. Ewers, J. (2002, September 16). Liza with a 3-year-old. *U. S. News and World Report*, p. 8.[166]

167. Moore LaRoe, L & Clark, R. (1997, May). La Salle's last voyage. *National Geographic*, *191*, 72.[167]

168. Gregory, S. (2003, February-March). Lewis and Clark: Explorers of the American West. *American Heritage*, *54*, 21.[168]

169. Etkin, J. (2003, April 21). Reclamation project; Leaving the vet for a new stadium in 2004, the Phillies are counting on fans - and victories - to return. *Rocky Mountain News*, p. 4H.[169]

170. Hadley, C. J. (1990, March). Savannah: Body and soul. *Saturday Evening Post, 262*, 82-7.[170]

171. Faber, A. (1980). *How to Talk So Kids Will Listen and Listen So Kids Will Talk*. New York: Avon Books, Inc., p. 94.[171]

172. Rand, A. (1971). *The Fountainhead*. New York: New American Library, p. 25.[172]

173. McKee, R. (1997). *Story: Substance, Structure, Style and the Principles of Screenwriting*. New York: Harper Publishers, p. 43.[173]

174. Nemeth, M. (2002, July 15). Disappearing Saskatchewan: As farmers abandon their land, they're taking small-town life with them. *Maclean's*, p. 18.[174]

175. Anderson, R. (2002, September). Decipher the past. *New Scientist. 175*, 52-4.[175]

176. Groff, Lauren (20008). *The Monsters of Templeton*. New York: Hyperion, p. 65.[176]

177. Rubenstein, H. (2003, May 1). Gather unto ye. *In Style, 10*, 101.[177]

178. Buckingham, M. (1999). *First, Break All the Rules: What the World's Greatest Managers Do Differently*. New York: Simon and Schuster, p. 185.[178]

179. Ricks, T. (1996, November). Hazardous duty: America's most decorated living soldier reports from the front and tells it the way it is. *Washington Monthly, 28*, 55.[179]

180. Feurer, A. (2001, May 13). Reporter's Notebook; Violent Acts Recalled, by a Man of Few Words. *New York Times*, sec. 1, p. 32.[180]

181. Goltz, T. (2003). *Chechnya Diary: A War Correspondent's Story of Surviving the War in Chechnya*. New York: Thomas Dunne Books, p. 166.[181]

182. Evans, E. (2002, October 18). "General" portrait incomplete. *The Houston Chronicle*, p. 01.[182]

183. Thompson, R. (2002, December 9). Football, Game 13, The Bills: Otis uses age-old tactics: Holds own with savvy, experience. *The Boston Herald*, p. O96.[183]

184. Covey, S. R. (1989). *Seven Habits of Highly Effective People*. New York: Simon and Schuster, Inc., p. 197.[184]

185. Wolff, A. (1994, May 30). An honest wage. *Sports Illustrated, 80*, 98.[185]

186. Doherty, M.S. (2000, October). Watermedia painting that outdoes Picasso. *American Artist, 64*, 70.[186]

187. Krakauer, J. (1997). *Eiger Dreams: Ventures among Men and Mountains*. New York: Anchor Books, p. 93.[187]

188. Perry, P. (1995, November-December). Teaching dogs new tricks. *Saturday Evening Post, 267*, 44-6.[188]

189. Fox, C. (2003, May 4). Architecture notes: A new name for GSU art school; Designation honors graduate. *The Atlanta Journal and Constitution*, p. 6M.[189]

190. Green, A. (2002, May 27). The magic basement. *The New Yorker, 78*, NA.[190]

191. Miller, H. (1989, May-June). Tracking the rich and famous. *Saturday Evening Post, 261*, 30.[191]

192. Patterson, Kerry; Joseph, Grenny; McMillan, Ron; and Switzler, Al (2002). *Crucial Conversations: Tools for Talking When Stakes are High*. New York: McGraw-Hill, p. 53. [192]

193. Browne, J. C. (1999). *The Sweet Potato Queens' Book of Love*. New York: Three Rivers Press, p. Back Matter.[193]

194. Pagels, E. (1989). *The Gnostic Gospels*. New York: Vintage Books, p. 152.[194]

195. Vogel, N. & Ingram C. (2003, February 9). Pleas make crisis personal. *Los Angeles Times*, p. 1.[195]

196. Prendergast, A. (2003, May 22). The long road home why so many parolees go back to prison, and how a new approach could help turn them around. *Denver Westward*, News/Featured Stories.[196]

197. Bryson, B. (2003). *A Short History of Nearly Everything*. New York: Random House, Inc., p. 347.[197]

198. Tolle, Eckhart (2008). *A New Earth: Awakening to Your Life's Purpose*. New York: Penguin Group, p. 19.[198]

199. Leo McKern Actor who shone with the Old Vic and at Stratford and won acclaim as Rumpole of the Bailey on television. (2002, July 24). *The Daily Telegraph*, p. 23.[199]

200. Cole, J. B. (2003). *This Day: Diaries from American Women*. Hillsboro, OR: Beyond Words Publishing, Inc., p. 146.[200]

201. Boylan, J. (2003, July). The memory artist. *O Magazine*, p. 183.[201]

202. Marklein, B. (2003, January 20). INS database worries colleges. *USA Today*, p. 6D.[202]

203. Grossberger, L. (2002, October 7). Hold on to your parts. *Mediaweek*, *12*, 34.[203]

204. Puig, C. (2003, March 21). Lunacy runs amok in "Dreamcatcher." *USA Today*, p. 10E.[204]

205. Ver Berkmoes, R. (1991, May-June). Tracking a killer: Why did seemingly healthy Amish babies suddenly sicken, become paralyzed, or die? Dr. Holmes Morton solved this mystery for the anguished parents. *Saturday Evening Post*, *263*, 58. [205]

206. Reid, T. R. (2003, May). The Sherpas. *National Geographic*, p. 60.[206]

207. Doyle D. P. & Pimentel, S. (1993, March). A study in change: Transforming the Charlotte-Mecklenburg schools. *Phi Delta Kappan*, *74*, 534-40.[207]

208. Friday Television. (2001, July 27). *The Guardian*, p.20.[208]

209. Toole, J. K. (1980). A Confederacy of Dunces. Broadway, NY: Grove Press, p. 362.[209]

210. Spock, B. (1992). *Dr. Spock's Baby and Childcare (7th Ed.)*. New York: Simon and Schuster, Inc., p. 43.[210]

211. Dolgun, A. (1975) *Alexander Dolgun's Story*. New York: Alfred A. Knopf, Inc, p. 4.[211]

212. Dolgun, A. (1975) *Alexander Dolgun's Story*. New York: Alfred A. Knopf, Inc., p. 60.[212]

213. Ban Breathnach, S. (1995). *Simple Abundance: A Daybook of Comfort and Joy*. New York: Warner Books, Inc., p. 102.[213]

214. Helfand, D. (2003, May 29). California; Bailout nears for Oakland schools. *Los Angeles Times*, California Metro, p. 1.[214]

215. Berger, E. (2003, May 4). Experts discuss nanotechnology for energy crisis. *The Houston Chronicle*, p.14A.[215]

216. Slywotzky, A. (2001, February 5). Standing tall in the tech slump: The dot-coms are collapsing around you. Don't gloat. Now's the time to remake your company. *Fortune*, *143*, 176.[216]

217. Bryson, B. (2003). *A Short History of Nearly Everything*. New York: Broadway Books, p. 82.[217]

218. Vinay Menon Television, Associated Press. (2003, May 29). Everest in need of rest after 50 years of hikers. *Toronto Star*, p. A26.[218]

219. Hillenbrand, L. (2001). *Seabiscuit: An American Legend*. New York: Random House, Inc., p. 202.[219]

220. Pressfield, D. (1998). *Gates of Fire*. New York: Bantam Doubleday Dell Publishing Group, Inc., p. 129.[220]

221. Nordlinger, J. (2003, January 27). Hootie vs. Hootie: The morality play surrounding Augusta National. *National Review*, 55. [221]

222. Collins, A. (2003). *The Draconomicon (Dungeons and Dragons)*. Renton, WA: Wizards of the Coast, Inc., p. 267.[222]

223. Newfield, J. (2002, October 7). The right's judicial juggernaut. *The Nation*, *275*, 11.[223]

224. The X-Factor: With its eagerly awaited Xbox, Microsoft gets into the videogame-console business. (2001, November 5). *Newsweek*, p. 40B.[224]

225. Service, R. (2003, April 6). Life and soul of the party. *Sunday Times*, Features, Culture, p. 39.[225]

226. Woods, A. (2003, April 12). Elegia: Works by JS Bach, JC Bach, Biber, Blow, Purcell etc. White: Les Voix Baroques. *Music Week*, p. 24.[226]

227. Winter, J. (1998, November). A taste of ashes. *History Today*, p. 8.[227]

228. Sragow, M. (2003, May 14). Another whirl: Still stylish, but talky, "Matrix Re-loaded" mostly runs in circles, killing time until the next sequel. *The Baltimore Sun*, p.1E..[228]

229. Sevitt, D. (2002, July 14). Photographers remember a "mentor." Famous portraitist loved to foster young talent. *Ottawa Citizen*, p. A5.[229]

230. Williams, D. (2002, August 5). The winning formula: For supercoach Ric Charlesworth, being the best in sport or business is more about doggedness than dazzle. *Time International, 160*, 50.[230]

231. Hope, C. (2003, May 3). Cruickshank has developed knack of reaching the annual meetings that others cannot reach. *The Herald*, p. 23.[231]

232. Kelleher, T. (1997, May 5). Jack Paar: As I was saying.... *People Weekly, 47*, 17.[232]

233. Chang, Jun (2003). *Wild Swans: Three Daughters of China*. New York: Touchstone, p. 496.[233]

234. Murphy, A. (1991, December 21). The grate one. *Sports Illustrated, 75*, 42-7.[234]

235. Cameron, W. B. (2003, February 8). A little "battle kill" nothing to fear. *Rocky Mountain News*, p. E2.[235]

236. Rauch, J. (2003, March). Caring for your introvert: The habits and needs of a little-understood group. (Personal File). *The Atlantic Monthly, 291*, 133-5.[236]

237. Cockburn, A. (2000, April). Yemen United. *National Geographic, 197*, 30.[237]

238. McGee, Harold (2004). *On Food and Cooking: The Science and Lore of the Kitchen*. New York: Scribner, p. 338.[238]

239. Bird, M. (2002, December 2). Death coast: After an aging tanker sinks off Spain, a vast slick of fuel oil destroys beaches, wildlife and fishermen's dreams. Could this disaster have been prevented? *Time International, 160*, 60.[239]

240. Dolgun, A. (1975) *Alexander Dolgun's Story*. New York: Alfred A. Knopf, Inc., p. 185.[240]

241. Fischel, M. (2002, September 27). Brother, can you spare a dime? *The Jerusalem Post*, Features, p. 4.[241]

242. Hitchens, C. (2002, April). The medals of his defeats: Our author takes the great man down a peg or two—and still finds that Churchill was a great man. *The Atlantic Monthly, 289*, 118-138.[242]

243. Amore, D. (2003, April 20). Contreras sent down. Pitcher needs time to adjust, regain confidence. Yankees notebook. *Hartford Courant*, p. E11.[243]

244. Baca, R. (2002, May 23). Weekend to remember: Art shows kick off three days of fests, reflections. *The Denver Post*, p. FF-01.[244]

245. Speelman, J. (2002, October 6). Escape, Games, Chess. *The Observer*, p. 19.[245]

246. Pollan, M. (2001). *The Botany of Desire: A Plant's-Eye View of the World*. New York: Random House, p. 85.[246]

247. Gen, B. (2003, May 17). Salazar vs. the gerrymander. *The Denver Post*, p. B-23.[247]

248. Jones, T. (2003, March 16). Atlantic 10: Dayton 79 Temple 72; Flyers find winning recipe, turn back tough owls for title. *Columbus Dispatch*, p. 04E.[248]

249. James, B. (2003, May 21). County is struggling to find coaches. *St. Petersburg Times*, p. 6.[249]

250. Bonilla, D. & Martin, H. (2003, May 23). Los Angeles: Little drop-off seen in Memorial Day travel. *Los Angeles Times*, p. 3.[250]

251. Dolgun, A. (1975) *Alexander Dolgun's Story*. New York: Alfred A. Knopf, Inc., p. 75.[251]

252. Her fiercest foe: America's first woman vice presidential candidate wages her toughest campaign—against a deadly cancer. (2001, September 17). *People Weekly*, p. 192.[252]

253. Wallach, J. (1999). *Desert Queen: The Extraordinary Life of Gertrude Bell: Adventurer, Adviser to Kings, Ally of Lawrence of Arabia*. New York: Anchor Books, p. 299.[253]

254. Daidoji, Y. (1999). *Code of the Samurai: A Modern Translation of the Bushido Shoshinsu*. Boston: Tuttle Publishing, p.6.[254]

255. Powers, A. (1999, June 28). Godfather of soul delivers a spectacle (Pop Review). *New York Times*, p. E1.[255]

256. Chen, D. W. (2000, June 23). House auctions gain favor in an eBay world. *New York Times*, p. A1.[256]

257. Friedman, G. & Lebard, M. (1992, May-June). Irreconcilable differences. *Psychology Today*, *25*, 48-52.[257]

258. Kidder, R. M. (1995). *How Good People Make Tough Choices: Resolving the Dilemmas of Ethical Living*. New York: Fireside, p. 80.[258]

259. Faber, M. (2002). *The Crimson Petal and the White*. Orlando, FL: Harcourt, p. 42.[259]

260. Miller, S. & Brailsford, K. (2000, May 22). A Jar of Hope, to go: Cancer survivor Vincene Parrinello cooks up creams that help save sick skin. *People Weekly*, *53*, 125.[260]

261. Petroski, H. (1992) *To Engineer Is Human: The Role of Failure in Successful Design*. New York: Vintage Books, p. 181.[261]

262. Menand, L. (2002, September 16). Faith, hope, and clarity. *The New Yorker*, *78*, p. NA.[262]

263. West, J. L. (2000, Spring). Annotating Mr. Fitzgerald. *American Scholar*, *69*, 82.[263]

264. Rau, J. (2003, May 1). Can Pataki win back allies? Rift widens as governor, Senate follow different agendas. *Newsday*, p. A22.[264]

265. Friedman, T. L. (2000). *The Lexus and the Olive Tree: Understanding Globalization*. New York: Random House, Inc., p. 436.[265]

266. Langworthy, D. (1996, September). Inside the tent. *American Theatre*, *13*, 17.[266]

267. Abbey, E. (1968). *Desert Solitaire*. New York: Ballantine Books, p. 150.[267]

268. Semler, G. (1995, September 25). A year in Iberia. *Forbes*, *156*, S95-101.[268]

269. James, C. (1984, April). A field linguist who lived his life for his subjects. *Smithsonian*, *15*, 153-66.[269]

270. Hedges, C. (2002). *War Is a Force that Gives Us Meaning*. New York: Anchor Books, p. 1.[270]

271. Langer, R. (2003, April). Where a pill won't reach: how to get drugs where they need to go. *Scientific American*, *288*, 50-8.[271]

272. Shilling, J. (2001, September 17). Perhaps the power of music is that it conveys on our behalf feelings to which the access of language is limited. *The Times, Features*.[272]

273. Curtin, N. (2003, February 10). Statesman and strategist. *America*, *188*, 26.[273]

274. Geer, P. (2002). *Simon's Saga for the SAT I Verbal*. Hauppauge, NY: Barron's Educational Series, Inc., p. 135.[274]

275. Sebold, A. (2002). *The Lovely Bones*. USA: Alice Sebold, p. 27.[275]

276. Ward, R. (2003, March-April). Moody teens: A diagnosis, but no cure. *Psychology Today*, *36*, 24.[276]

277. Sellers, P. (2003, May 26). Ted Turner is a worried man. His media career is gone with the wind. His faith in the United Nations looks naive. He thinks humanity's on the verge of extinction, and he's down to his last billion. *Fortune*, *147*, 124.[277]

278. Builder named to Order of Canada. (2003, April 26). *Toronto Star*, p. J06.[278]

279. Shapiro, M. (2003). *The Last Good Season: Brooklyn, the Dodgers, and Their Final Pennant Race Together*. USA: Doubleday, p. 62.[279]

280. Doyle, A. C. (2002). *The Complete Sherlock Holmes*. New York: Gramercy Books, p. 427.[280]

281. Christman, E. (1998, August 8). Alliance to exit chapter 11. *Billboard*, *110*, 6.[281]

282. Tiffany, L. (1998, September). Shop around. *Entrepreneur*, *26*, 192D.[282]

283. Hopper, A. (2002, December 12). Alice's adventures in wonderland: Christmas review: Keswick. *The Stage*, p. 22.[283]

284. Kotter, J. P. (1996) *Leading Change*. Cambridge, MA: Harvard Business School Press, p. 3.[284]

285. Armstrong, K. (1993). *A History of God: The 4,000-Year Quest of Judaism, Christianity and Islam*. New York: Ballatine Books, p. 297.[285]

286. Robson, B. (2003, May 28). Hargrove's "RH Factor": Mixing in some new blood. *The Washington Post*, p. C05.[286]

287. Pence, A. (2003 February 19). Not all orchids are difficult to care for. *The San Francisco Chronicle*, p. 6WB.[287]

288. Klawans, S. (2002, September). The play's the thing. *The Nation*, *275*, 44.[288]

289. Grossberger, L. (2003, May 12). Will endorse for food. *Mediaweek*, *13*, 44.[289]

290. Elliott, C. (2001, July). Samuel Pepys' London chronicles: The candid diarist portrays the ravages of fire and plague, the bawdy court of Charles II, and his own romps with maids. *Smithsonian*, p. 102.[290]

291. Ver Berkmoes, R. (1991, May-June). Tracking a killer: Why did seemingly healthy Amish babies suddenly sicken, become paralyzed, or die? Dr. Holmes Morton solved this mystery for the anguished parents. *Saturday Evening Post, 263*, 58-64.[291]

292. How to get ordinary investors back into the market. (2003, March 31). *Business Week*, p.12.[292]

293. Chu, D. (1986, June 9). Rice isn't just for weddings: Judy Moscovitz used it to diet from 275 lbs. to a svelte 123. *People Weekly*, p. 133.[293]

294. Senge, P. M. (1990). *The Fifth Discipline*. New York: Bantam Doubleday Dell Publishing Group, p. 295.[294]

295. Rosen, M. (1993, June 21). The Rivers run together: After a period of estrangement, Joan Rivers and daughter Melissa share life, laughs and love. *People Weekly, 39*, 70-6.[295]

296. Sheppard, R. (2003, March 24). Cracking the genetic code: It's 50 years since two brash, ambitious scientists unveiled the double helix. *Maclean's*, p. 48.[296]

297. Engardio, J. (2000, January 5). Charity begins @ home; A young software engineer has a plan to teach Silicon Valley to change its tightfisted ways. *SF Weekly*, Features.[297]

298. Brandt, A. (1997, February 24). One connected quartet. *Forbes, 159*, S65-76.[298]

299. Mark Verstegen, M. (2004). *Core Performance: The Revolutionary Workout Program to Transform Your Body and Your Life*. USA: Rodale, p. 68.[299]

300. Calloway, C. G. (1994). *The World Turned Upside Down: Indian Voices from Early America (The Bedford Series in History and Culture)*. Boston: Bedford Books, p. 68.[300]

301. Collins, A., Willisams, S. & Wyatt J. (1993). *The Draconomicon (Dungeons and Dragons)*. Renton, WA: Wizards of the Coast, Inc., p. 264.[301]

302. Cialdini, R. B. (1993). *Influence: The Psychology of Persuasion*. New York: Wlliam Morrow and Company, Inc., p. Back Matter.[302]

303. McLean, A. (2003). *Investing in Real Estate*. Hoboken, NJ: John Wiley and Sons, Inc., p. 21.[303]

304. McCafferty, M. (2003). *Second Helpings*. New York: Three Rivers Press, p. 178.[304]

305. Tozer, T. (1996, May-June). Letting Michael be Michael ... a 12-year-old with 4 Guinness records. *Saturday Evening Post*, p. 268.[305]

306. Platoni, K. (2003, June). Great expectations. *Smithsonian*, p. 61.[306]

307. Hillenbrand, L. (2001). *Seabiscuit: An American Legend*. New York: Random House, Inc., p. 366.[307]

308. McKee, R. (1997). *Story: Substance, Structure, Style and the Principles of Screenwriting*. New York: Harper Publishers, Inc., p. 27.[308]

309. McCullough, D. (2001). *The Great Bridge: The Epic Story of the Building of the Brooklyn Bridge*. New York: Simon & Schuster, chapter 1.[309]

310. McGee, Harold (2004). *On Food and Cooking: The Science and Lore of the Kitchen*. New York, p. 338.[310]

311. Biskupic, J. (2003, February 14). Dems: "We will not relent" on filibuster. *USA Today*, p. 7A.[311]

312. Camp, D. (1997, November 10). Renegade revolutionaries: A bitter strike reveals rifts in staid Ontario. *Maclean's*, p. 21.[312]

313. Neville, K. (1988). *The Eight*. New York: The Ballantine Publishing Group, p. 158.[313]

314. Roberts, C. (2004). *Founding Mothers: The Women Who Raised Our Nation*. New York: HarperCollins Publishers Inc., p. 32.[314]

315. Zinn, H. (2003). *A People's History of the United States: 1492-Present*. New York: HarperCollins Publishers Inc., p. 158.[315]

316. Sunny Jim just can't say no. (2003, May 23). *The Dominion Post* (Wellington, New Zealand), p. 2.[316]

317. Armstrong, K. (1993). *A History of God: The 4,000-Year Quest of Judaism, Christianity and Islam*. New York: Ballantine Books, p. 358.[317]

318. McElwaine, S. (1995, January-February). Newhouse. *Washington Monthly*, 27, 37.[318]

319. Weiss, B. (1988). *Many Lives, Many Masters*. New York: Simon and Schuster, Inc., p. 24.[319]

320. Van Gelder, L. (2002, April 2). Footlights. *New York Times*, p. E1.[320]

321. Levine, M. (2003). *The Myth of Laziness*. New York: Simon and Schuster, p.155.[321]

322. Larson, E. (2003). *The Devil in the White City: Murder, Magic, and Madness at the Fair That Changed America*. New York: Crown Publishers, p. 130.[322]

323. Fields-Meyer, T. (1996, June 24). Married to a stranger. *People Weekly*, 45, 48-52.[323]

324. Ambrose, S. (1996). *Undaunted Courage: Meriwether Lewis Thomas Jefferson and the Opening of the American West*. New York: Touchstone, p. 372.[324]

325. Ellis, J. J. (2000). *Founding Brothers: The Revolutionary Generation*. New York: Alfred A. Knopf, p. 201.[325]

326. Dirda, M. (2002, July-August). Great Granny Webster. *The Atlantic Monthly*, 290, 189.[326]

327. Ross, B. (2002, December 24). Sailor "Antwone Fisher" charts a new course in life. *Tampa Tribune*, Baylife, p. 8.[327]

328. Clothier, S. (2002). *Bones Would Rain From the Sky: Deepening Our Relationships with Dogs*. New York: Warner Books, p. 235.[328]

329. Prose, F. (1997, April 14). After the madness: A judge's own prison memoir. *People Weekly*, 47, 35.[329]

330. Bornstein, D. (2004). *How to Change the World: Social Entrepreneurs and the Power of New Ideas*. New York: Oxford University Press, Inc., p. 44.[330]

331. Rowden, T. (2003, April 17). Fredeking and Arnold await appeal outcome; Former police chief was fired in 2001. *St. Louis Post-Dispatch*, Jefferson County Post, p. 1.[331]

332. McCallum, J. (2000, August 14). Unflagging: Five-time gold medalist Jenny Thompson, 27, plans to undress her younger rivals in Sydney and become the most decorated U.S. woman Olympian ever. *Sports Illustrated*, 93, 52.[332]

333. Cobo, L. (2002, May 11). Leading in nominations, Lupillo Rivera is proving that everything old is new again. *Billboard*, 114, p. LM-12.[333]

334. Gladwell, M. (2002). *The Tipping Point: How Little Things Can Make a Big Difference*. USA: Little, Brown and Company, p. 92.[334]

335. Phillips, B. (1999). *Body for Life: 12 Weeks to Mental and Physical Strength*. New York: HarperCollins, p. 74.[335]

336. Anderson, W. (1989, July-August). In the footsteps of the Lincolns. *Saturday Evening Post*, 261, 64.[336]

337. Dolgun, A. (1975) *Alexander Dolgun's Story*. New York: Alfred A. Knopf, Inc., p. 25.[337]

338. Derek, C. B. (2001). The effect of admissions test preparation: Evidence from NELS: 88. *Chance*, 14, 10.[338]

339. De Tocqueville, A. (1984). *Democracy in America*. New York: Penguin Putnam, Inc., p. 43.[339]

340. Murphy, J. (2000). *The Power of Your Subconscious Mind*. New York: Reward Books, p. 218.[340]

341. Greenblatt, A. (2003, May). Tear down this wall. *Washington Monthly*, 35, 56-8.[341]

342. Jackman, T. (2003, February 13). Malvo attorneys ask court for 5 investigators. *The Washington Post*, p. B03.[342]

343. Waldrop, M. (1986, April 4). The currents of space. *Science*, 232, 26.[343]

344. Dillman, L. (2003, February 3). Tennis: Who knew the places he'd go. *Los Angeles Times*, Sports, Part 4, p. 8.[344]

345. Liss, D. (2000). *A Conspiracy of Paper*. New York: The Ballantine Publishing Group, p. 150.[345]

346. Carnegie, D. (1956). *How to Develop Self-Confidence and Influence People*. New York: Simon and Schuster Inc., p. 55.[346]

347. Jacobson, A. (2003, May 20). Out of the shadow. *Newsday*, p. B06.[347]

348. Simon, J. (1996, September 30). A little lower than festive. *National Review, 48,* 67.[348]

349. Eire, C. (2003). *Waiting for Snow in Havana: Confessions of a Cuban Boy.* New York: The Free Press, p. 102.[349]

350. Peck, M. S. (2003). *The Road Less Traveled, 25th Anniversary Edition: A New Psychology of Love, Traditional Values and Spiritual Growth.* New York: Simon and Schuster, Inc., p. 137.[350]

351. Peters, T. (1994). *The Pursuit of Wow!* New York: Random House, p. 69.[351]

352. Kaushik, Avinash (2007). *Web Analytics: An Hour a Day.* Indianapolis, IN: Wiley Publishing Inc., p. 223.[352]

353. Fields-Meyer, T. (1999, December 20). Dead end: A moment of anger in rush-hour traffic costs the life of a mother of three. *People Weekly, 52,* 131.[353]

354. Moss, E. L. (2000, January). How drawing and driving are alike. *American Artist, 64,* 42.[354]

355. Mehta, N. (2002, November 12, 2002). Tour lends deeper appreciation for outside world. *Albuquerque Journal.* Retrieved December 22, 2003, from http://www.abqjournal.com/news/yes/797610fun11-12-02.htm[355]

356. Tolle, Eckhart (2208). *A New Earth: Awakening to Your Life's Purpose.* New York: Penguin Group, p.169.[356]

357. Loehr, J. (2003). *The Power of Full Engagement: Managing Energy, Not Time, is the Key to High Performance and Personal Renewal.* New York: Free Press, p. 82.[357]

358. Krakauer, J. (2003). *Under the Banner of Heaven: A Story of Violent Faith.* New York: Doubleday, p. 325.[358]

359. Wilks, Eileen (2005). *Mortal Danger (The World of the Lupi, Book 2).* The Berkley Publishing Group, p. 125.[359]

360. Ross, S. (2003, April 27). Marty all class in le scandale. *Daily News,* p. 66.[360]

361. Kreiter, T. (1997, May-June). Salt savvy. *Saturday Evening Post, 269,* 26.[361]

362. Lawlet, A. (2003, June). Iraq's treasures. *Smithsonian,* p. 49.[362]

363. Bennett, B. (2001, July 16). Annals of conservatism: We are all God's creatures—yes, even the pigeons. *Time International, 158,* 10.[363]

364. Hilton, M. (2000, May). Smoking gun. *History Today, 50,* 36.[364]

365. Rodman, S. (2003, April 4). Music: The kids are alright. Rockers' offspring take center stage. *The Boston Herald,* p. S03.[365]

366. McCullough, D. (1992). *Truman.* New York: Simon and Schuster, p. 357.[366]

367. Millard, C. (1999, September). Hunting with eagles in the mountains of Mongolia. *National Geographic, 196,* 90.[367]

368. Scherzer, B. (2000, March 6). Magic carpet ride. *Variety, 378,* 70.[368]

369. Lawlet, A. (2003, June). Iraq's treasures. *Smithsonian,* p. 53.[369]

370. Hoffer, R. (1999, January 18). Haunted. *Sports Illustrated, 90,* 62.[370]

371. Ronis, A. (2003, May 20). Mary Louis tops Molloy. *Newsday,* p. A69.[371]

372. Dorgan, E. (2000, September). Cents and sensibility. *American Heritage, 51,* 74.[372]

373. Devil Rays to test Piniella's patience: Leading off players to watch spotlight battle: Chicago connection the lineup numbers game. (2003, March 14). *Chicago Sun-Times,* p. 140.[373]

374. Bergman, B. (1998, October 12). Show-no-mercy-Mercer: In his new show, Rick Mercer once again plays it nasty. *Maclean's, 111,* 73.[374]

375. Communities. (2003, April 17). *Plain Dealer,* p. B3.[375]

376. McClure, S. (2002, August 24). Hyde out. (Global Music Pulse). *Billboard, 114,* 57.[376]

377. Sherman, M. (2003, March 7). Visa takes measures to curb identity theft: Credit-card companies to require new machines to display only four digits. *The Gazette,* p. B2.[377]

378. Schneier, B. (2000). *Secrets and Lies: Digital Security in a Networked World.* New York: John Wiley and Sons, Inc., p.209.[378]

379. Vonnegut, K. (1968). *Welcome to the Monkey House*. New York: Dell Publishing, p.72.[370]

380. Schrade, B. (2000, September 13). Cobb school conduct code on agenda today. *The Atlantic Journal and Constitution*, p. B3.[380]

381. Law unto himself. (2003, April 4). *The Times* (London), p. 23.[381]

382. Engelmann, P. (2002, December 15). Kirkland, Martha. An inconvenient heir. *Booklist*, *99*, 738.[382]

383. Sehlinger, B. (2003). *The Unofficial Guide to Walt Disney World 2004*. Hoboken, NJ: John Wiley and Sons, Inc., p. 503.[383]

384. Boyle, T.C. (2003, April 6). Colony of dreamers. *Sunday Times* (London), p. 47.[384]

385. Eggers, D. (2001). *A Heartbreaking Work of Staggering Genius*. New York: Random House, p. 316.[385]

386. Blevins, J. (2003, May 27). Sweet venture tastes great, less ingredients Denverite's nutrition bars a natural passion for unprocessed, healthy and, yes, tasty food inspired successful creation. *The Denver Post*, p. C-01.[386]

387. Ross, D. (1992, September-October). The patient who couldn't speak. *Saturday Evening Post*, *264*, 64.[387]

388. Underhill, P. (1999). *Why We Buy: The Science Of Shopping*. New York: Simon and Schuster, p. 68.[388]

389. Gillen, M. (2000, September 9). UMG, MP3 court case hinges on "willfulness." *Billboard*, p. 112.[389]

390. Fernandez-Armesto, F. (1996, March). Times and tides. *History Today*, *46*, 4.[390]

391. Thompson, H. S. (1995). *Hell's Angels*. New York: Ballantine Books, p. 233.[391]

392. Ford, D. (2003, May 2). Community; Group helps young Jews help others. *The San Francisco Chronicle*, p. 1.[392]

393. Grall, G. (1999, April). The pools of spring. *National Geographic*, *195*, 122.[393]

394. Wilson, B. (2002, August). Like his women, Picasso's apples are splayed open, chopped around. *New Statesman*, *131*, 40.[394]

395. Eldredge, J. (2001). *Wild at Heart: Discovering the Secret of a Man's Soul.* Nashville, TN: Thomas Nelson, Inc. p. 4.[395]

396. Oppelarre, J. (2002, December 2). Wal-Mart: Hicks mix with pix. Store-struck Hollywood kowtows to retail leviathan. *Variety*, *389*, 1.[396]

397. Lane, A. (2002, August 12). Field trip. *New Yorker*.[397]

398. Leach, M. (2003, June 15). Tough Romans Apparently Liked Flowers. *Columbus Dispatch*, p. 01I.[398]

399. Shaughnessy, D. (2003, May 21). It seems that Lyon has closed in on the job. *The Boston Globe*, p. F5.[399]

400. Kreisman, J. J. (1989). *I Hate You, Don't Leave Me: Understanding the Borderline Personality*. Los Angeles: Price Stern Sloan, Inc., p. 106.[400]

Bibliography

Atkinson, R. C. (1975). Mnemotechnics in second-language learning. *American Psychologist, 30,* 821-828.

Avila, E. & Sadoski, M. (1996). Exploring new applications of the keyword method to acquire English vocabulary. *Language Learning, 46,* 379-395.

Carney, R. N. & Levin, J. R. (1998). Coming to term with the keyword method in Introductory Psychology: A "neuromnemonic" example. *Teaching of Psychology, 25,*132-134.

Harper Collins Webster's Dictionary. (2003). New York: Harper Collins Publishers.

Jones, M. J., Levin, M. E., Levin, J.R. & Beitzel, B.D. (2000). Can vocabulary-learning strategies and pair-learning formats be profitably combined? *Journal of Educational Psychology, 92,* 256-262.

Levin, J. R. (1982). Pictures as prose learning devices. In A. Flammer & W. Kintsch (ed.). *Discourse Processing-Advances in Psychology.* New York: North-Holland Publishing Company. p. 412-444.

Levin, J. R. (1986). Four cognitive principles of learning-strategy instruction. *Educational Psychologist, 21,* 3-17.

Levin, J. R. (1983). Pictorial strategies for school learning:Practical illustrations. In M. Pressley & J.R. Levin (Eds.), *Cognitive strategy research: Educational applications* (pp. 213-237). New York: Springer-Verlag.

Levin, J.R. (1981). The Mnemonic'80s: Keywords in the classroom. *Educational Psychologist, 16,* 65-82.

Lysynchuk, L. & Pressley, M. (1990). Vocabulary (ch.4) in *Cognitive strategy instruction that really improves children's academic performance.* Cabridge, MA: Brookline Books.

Mastropieri, M. A. & Scruggs, T. E. (1991). *Teaching students ways to remember.* BrooklineBooks: Cambridge, MA.

Merriam Webster's online dictionary. Retrieved from www.merriamwebster.com.

Procter, P. (Ed.). (1995). *Cambridge International Dictionary of English.* Cambridge. United Kingdom: Cambridge University Press.

Sternberg, R. J. (1986) Beyond IQ: *A triarchic theory of Human inteligence.* Yale University Press: New Haven, CT.

The American Heritage Dictionary. (2001). Boston, NY: Houghton Mifflin Company.

Wang, A. Y. & Thomas, H. T. (1995). Effect of keywords on long-term retention: Help or hindrance? *Journal of Educational Psychology, 87,* 468-475.

Answer Key

Review Answers

Section 1

Crossword Puzzle
Across: 6-Belittle 8-Aberration 10-Amiable 12-Austere 13-Assail 7-Antagonist 20-Abstruse

Down: 1-Baleful 2-Aesthetic 3-Abstinence 4-Arbiter 5-Animosity 7-Belie 9-Amalgamate 11-Ameliorate 14-Affinity 15-Abet 16-Aloof 18-Acquiesce 19-Atrophy

Multiple Choice
1-c. baleful 2-d. abstruse 3-a. animosity 4-b. abstinence 5-d. atrophy 6-a. aesthetic 7-b. aberration 8-c. antagonist 9-a. belie 10-d. austere 11-d. abetted 12-b. amiable 13-d. aloof 14-c. affinity 15-b. ameliorated 16-d. assailed 17-a. acquiesced 18-d. belittle 19-c. arbiter 20-b. amalgamated

Matching
1-A 2-M 3-E 4-K 5-T 6-G 7-L 8-N 9-F 10-H 11-R 12-P 13-C 14-I 15-Q 16-B 17-J 18-D 19-O 20-S

Section 2

Crossword Puzzle
Across: 2-Copious 3-Crass 6-Chagrin 8-Composure 9-Cache 11-Blithe 12-Contrite 13-Countermand 15-Catalyst

Down: 1-Buffoon 3-Criterion 4-Bereft 5-Boor 6-Cajole 7-Bombastic 9-Capitulate 10-Covert 11-Broach 12-Conundrum 14-Daunt

Multiple Choice
1-c. broach 2-b. cajole 3-a. catalyst 4-b. chagrin 5-d. blithe 6-c. criteria 7-b. daunted 8-a. composure 9-d. boor 10-d. buffoon 11-b. contrite 12-a. bombastic 13-a. cache 14-c. conundrum 15-c. countermanded 16-b. bereft 17-d. covert 18-c. copious 19-a. crass 20-b. capitulated

Matching
1-E 2-N 3-I 4-K 5-L 6-Q 7-F 8-G 9-B 10-C 11-J 12-H 13-M 14-P 15-T 16-O 17-R 18-D 19-A 20-S

Section 3

Crossword Puzzle

Across: 2-Deference 3-Demur 6-Debacle 7-Decadence 9-Diffuse 10-Dearth 11-Derogatory 13-Diffidence 14-Despot 15-Diatribe 16-Disparity

Down: 1-Deprecate 3-Docile 4-Delineate 5-Disposition 8-Discordant 9-Dormant 12-Demagogue 14-Distraught 15-Dilatory

Multiple Choice

1-a. disparity 2-b. dearth 3-a. delineates 4-c. decadence 5-b. demagogue 6-a. docile 7-d. demurred 8-c. despots 9-d. derogatory 10-a. diffused 11-b. diatribe 12-b. diffidence 13-b. dilatory 14-c. deprecating 15-d. distraught 16-d. discordant 17-d. debacle 18-c. disposition 19-a. dormant 20-c. deference

Matching

1-N 2-C 3-H 4-A 5-O 6-K 7-F 8-R 9-M 10-G 11-Q 12-T 13-E 14-P 15-B 16-J 17-S 18-I 19-D 20-L

Section 4

Crossword Puzzle

Across: 3-Epilogue 6-Exacerbate 8-Fastidious 9-Exonerate 11-Extricate 15-Encumber 16-Embroil 17-Exhortation

Down: 1-Fallacious 2-Elucidate 3-Enervate 4-Evanescent 5-Erudite 7-Efficacious 10-Enhance 11-Expunge 12-Eclectic 13-Enigma 14-Fabricate 16-Eulogy

Multiple Choice

1-d.expunged 2-a.encumbered 3-c. eclectic 4-c. exacerbated 5-a. efficacious 6-a.fastidious 7-b. exonerated 8-a. embroiled 9-d. enhanced 10-b. enigma 11-a. fallacious 12-d. erudite 13-b. evanescent 14-a. exhortation 15-b. elucidated 16-c. extricate 17-d. fabricated 18-b. epilogue 19-c. enervated 20-c. eulogize

Matching

1-Q 2-D 3-T 4-S 5-J 6-M 7-K 8-A 9-C 10-H 11-F 12-I 13-O 14-N 15-E 16-B 17-P 18-L 19-R 20-G

Section 5

Crossword Puzzle

Across: 2-Garrulous 3-Hone 7-Gratuitous 9-Hyperbole
10-Imprecation 12-Impassive 13-Fledgling 15-Flagrant 16-Gall

Down: 1-Foment 4-Feckless 5-Guile 6-Fervor 8-Hapless
9-Hackneyed 10-Immaterial 11-Impervious 13-Fortuitous
14-Garner 15-Forestall

Multiple Choice

1-a. imprecations 2-b. fervor 3-b. forestall 4-a. feckless
5-b. hapless 6-c. fortuitous 7-d. gall 8-b. impervious 9-a. garner
10-b. garrulous 11-c. gratuitous 12-a. fomented 13-c. impassive
14-d. guile 15-a. hackneyed 16-c. hone 17-d. hyperboles
18-d. fledgling 19-d. immaterial 20-c. flagrant

Matching

1-L 2-M 3-J 4-S 5-A 6-Q 7-E 8-H 9-P 10-G 11-I 12-K
13-F 14-R 15-D 16-O 17-C 18-T 19-B 20-N

Section 6

Crossword Puzzle

Across: 3-Inane 6-Ingenuous 8-Inadvertent 9-Irascible 12-Mar
14-Indolent 15-Loquacious 17-Indefatigable 18-Intrepid

Down: 1-Lionize 2-Inure 4-Insipid 5-Judicious 7-Lachrymose
10-Intractable 11-Lassitude 12-Maladroit 13-Lugubrious
14-Insolvent 16-Meager

Multiple Choice

1-a. insolvent 2-a. maladroit 3-d. indolent 4-d. lugubrious
5-b. inured 6-b. insipid 7-b. inadvertently 8-c. judicious
9-d. intractable 10-d. meager 11-a. irascible 12-c. lachrymose
13-b. lassitude 14-d. lionized 15-d. loquacious
16-c. indefatigable 17-b. marred 18-c. ingenuous 19-a. intrepid
20-d. inane

Matching

1-C 2-R 3-M 4-G 5-A 6-E 7-N 8-H 9-O 10-I 11-P 12-B
13-D or F 14-J 15-Q 16-K 17-F or D 18-S 19-L 20-T

Section 7

Crossword Puzzle
Across: 2-Phlegmatic 4-Nadir 5-Paradigm 9-Perfidious
11-Obscure 13-Permeable 15-Pariah 16-Philanthropic

Down: 1-Petulant 3-Mendicant 5-Pellucid 6-Multifarious
7-Officious 8-Negligible 9-Perspicacious 10-Opulent
11-Obstreperous 12-Pallid 13-Partisan 14-Morose

Multiple Choice
1-a. morose 2-d. phlegmatic 3-d. partisan 4-c. multifarious
5-c. nadir 6-c. perfidious 7-d. negligible 8-a. obscure 9-c. pariah
10-b. mendicants 11-b. obstreperous 12-b. permeable
13-b. opulent 14-c. pallid 15-d. paradigms 16-a. pellucid
17-c. perspicacious 18-d. petulant 19-a. philanthropic
20-b. officious

Matching
1-I 2-C 3-L 4-E 5-A 6-T 7-K 8-H 9-P 10-S 11-B
12-F 13-D 14-R 15-G 16-M 17-Q 18-O 19-N 20-J

Section 8

Crossword Puzzle
Across: 3-Quandary 5-Relic 8-Ponderous 9-Rancor
10-Pretentious 13-Profusion 14-Raze 16-Prevaricate

Down: 1-Protract 2-Precocious 4-Recluse 6-Propitious
7-Proselytize 8-Proclivity 11-Raconteur 12-Pugnacious
13-Pundit 14-Ramify 15-Placate 17-Rebuff

Multiple Choice
1-a. pretentious 2-d. relic 3-c. proclivity 4-b. rebuffed
5-a. propitious 6-b. prevaricated 7-c. protracted 8-d. pugnacious
9-c. ponderous 10-a. pundit 11-b. quandary 12-b. raconteur
13-d. rancor 14-b. placate 15-b. proselytize 16-a. razed
17-d. profusion 18-c. recluse 19-d. precocious 20-c. ramified

Matching
1-K 2-F 3-A 4-P 5-Q 6-S 7-E 8-J 9-B 10-H 11-C 12-D
13-G 14-N 15-R 16-O 17-T 18-M 19-L 20-I

Section 9

Crossword

Across: 3-Sequester 6-Scrutinize 7-Scoff 9-Ribald
12-Repudiate 13-Sophistry 14-Stymie 15-Substantiate
16-Salutary 17-Sanguine

Down: 1-Sporadic 2-Supersede 4-Superficial 5-Retrograde
8-Sagacity 10-Stultifying 11-Saturate 13-Sectarian 15-Sullen
16-Serendipity

Multiple Choice

1-d. sagacious 2-c. substantiated 3-a. retrograde 4-d. saturated
5-a. sequestered 6-c. ribald 7-b. sanguine 8-d. superficial
9-a. salutary 10-b. supersede 11-a. stymied 12-a. scoffed
13-c. sectarian 14-a. serendipity 15-b. sophistry 16-c. sporadic
17-d. stultifying 18-b. repudiated 19-d. sullen 20-b. scrutinizing

Matching Review

1-P 2-H 3-J 4-C 5-Q 6-M 7-S 8-A 9-E 10-I 11-T 12-N
13-F 14-K 15-R 16-L 17-D 18-G 19-O 20-B

Section 10

Crossword

Across: 3-Voluble 5-Thwart 6-Surreptitious 10-Transient
11-Voracious 13-Tirade 14- Turpitude 17-Zealot

Down: 1-Tenuous 2-Surmise 3-Vapid 4-Utopian 7-Untenable
8-Wither 9-Writhe 10-Truncate 11-Verbose 12-Sycophant
15-Talon 16-Vilify

Multiple Choice

1-c. thwart 2-a. vapid 3-b. surreptitious 4-a. voracious
5-d. talons 6-a. surmised 7-b. tenuous 8-c. sycophant
9-d. transient 10-b. verbose 11-a. truncates 12-b. withered
13-b. turpitude 14-d. zealous 15-c. untenable 16-b. tirade
17-c. writhing 18-d. utopian 19-c. vilified 20-d. voluble

Matching

1-E 2-P 3-S 4-T 5-B 6-C 7-A 8-D 9-F 10-I 11-J 12-K 13-L
14-M 15-N 16-G 17-Q 18-R 19-O 20-H

Index

Introduction

words

Free Audio

O N L I N E

http://solida.net/

VOCABBUSTERS

study style

Make

SOLID A

vocabulary
f u n ,
meaningful
&
memorable

Dusti D. Howell, Ph.D.
Deanne Howell, M.S.

www.ingramcontent.com/pod-product-compliance
Lightning Source LLC
LaVergne TN
LVHW051622080426
835511LV00016B/2122